WRITING

A Content Approach To ESL Composition

BOWNESS HIGH SCHOOL
4627 - 77 STREET N.W.
CALGARY, AB T3B 2N6

ESL

WRITING

A Content Approach To ESL Composition

MARK JENKINS
Monterey Peninsula College

PRENTICE HALL REGENTS, Upper Saddle River, New Jersey 07458

Library of Congress Cataloging-in-Publication Data

JENKINS, MARK (MARK G.)
   Writing, a content approach to ESL composition.

   Includes index.
   1. English language—Text-books for foreign speakers.
I. Title.
PE1128.J43 1986   808'.042   85-16727
ISBN 0-13-969544-3

Editorial/production supervision and
   interior design: Dee Amir Josephson
Cover design: Wanda Lubelska
Manufacturing buyer: Harry P. Baisley

© 1986 by Prentice-Hall Regents
Prentice-Hall, Inc.
A Simon & Schuster Company
Upper Saddle River, New Jersey 07458

Printed in the United States of America

10

ISBN 0-13-969544-3

Prentice-Hall International (UK) Limited, *London*
Prentice-Hall of Australia Pty. Limited, *Sydney*
Prentice-Hall Canada Inc., *Toronto*
Prentice-Hall Hispanoamericana, S.A., *Mexico*
Prentice-Hall of India Private Limited, *New Delhi*
Prentice-Hall of Japan, Inc., *Tokyo*
Simon & Schuster Asia Pte. Ltd., *Singapore*
Editora Prentice-Hall do Brasil, Ltda., *Rio de Janeiro*

To My Parents

CONTENTS

Lesson 5   **Paraphrasing and Explaining a Process**
Subject: Physiology and Biology   81

Lesson 6   **Dividing Information**
Subject: Computer Applications   99

PREFACE

AUDIENCE

This book is for high-intermediate or advanced ESL composition students in either an intensive program or an ESL freshman composition course. It is best suited for students with TOEFL scores between 460 and 500, students who are making, or are about to make, the transition to academic life.

Teachers with classes closer to TOEFL 460 than TOEFL 500 will probably not try to finish the book, which contains more than most classes can cover in one semester. Teachers with stronger classes may choose to begin with a later lesson, an option which is feasible because the major rhetorical points in the first three lessons are repeated in later lessons, as outlined in the *Teacher's Manual*.

APPROACH

This text is built on the idea that the problems of writing, the problems of process and form, can best be understood in relation to specific content. The process of academic writing is viewed as one in which the writer must engage, understand, and manipulate ideas and information; and form is presented as an ordering of content, rather than as a set of conventions to be followed or molds to be filled.

Grammar, too, is taught in connection with content and as needed for specific writing tasks. Throughout the book grammar and rhetoric are given roughly equal weight: Only teachers are tempted to see grammar and writing as separable; students never do.

SEQUENCE

The sequence of materials in this book reflects the fact that students at the lower end of the scale mentioned (TOEFL 460–500) are often making the transition to academic English, and more generally, to academic ways of thinking. The topics in the first four lessons are therefore based on personal experience, or previous knowledge, and assume a lower level of grammatical sophistication than the remaining six lessons, which are less personal and more academic in content.

FORMAT

Each lesson consists of four parts. In *Cycle One* the student is introduced to the general content of the lesson and practices two or three of the points—grammatical or rhetorical—that are important to the lesson. In *Cycle Two,* to maintain interest, there is usually a shift to a new but related topic. Two or three new points—again, grammatical or rhetorical—are taught in this section, which concludes with a directed writing. The third section, *Adding On,* introduces a variety of new points which will be of use in writing the final essay of the lesson, for which suggested topics are given in the fourth section, *Additional Writing Topics.*

The format is cyclical, or layered: An important point may be practiced several times in a single lesson, as well as reviewed in a later lesson.

TEACHER'S MANUAL

The teacher's manual offers specific suggestions on using this book, provides background information on some of the topics, and contains answers to most exercises.

ACKNOWLEDGEMENTS

I would like to thank the students who used and responded to these lessons in so many earlier versions: Their reactions gave these materials their final form. I would also like to give my special thanks to Jan Thoele for patiently testing and constructively criticizing those earlier versions.

WRITING

A Content Approach
To ESL Composition

Lesson 1

WRITING A PERSONAL ESSAY

Subject: University and Job Applications

Contents:

INTRODUCTION

This beginning lesson will introduce you to the most basic questions a writer must ask: What is the purpose of a specific piece of writing? Who is it being written for? What does this reader know about the topic? What kind of information should be included in a particular essay? How does the writer gather information? How can this information be organized?

In Cycle One you will read and analyze an essay written by a Chinese woman as part of her application to an American university. You will consider why she was asked to write this essay and who she wrote it for. You will see what information about herself she considered appropriate or useful and how she organized it.

In Cycle Two you will write a personal essay of your own. The special emphasis in this section is on gathering, selecting, and organizing information.

The third section, Adding On, introduces a number of additional points on grammar and organization. The exercises will help you begin to develop a clear, efficient style.

CYCLE ONE

Practice 1. Reading

The following essay was written as part of an application to the University of California. The student who wrote it was following these directions in the application form:

You must enclose a personal essay along with the application form. You are encouraged to write about things that are important to you and tell about yourself. Topics might include your community service, awards you have received, class and student body offices you have held, school activities (such as athletics, dramatics, journalism, musical performances), work experience, educational interests and goals, personal career expectations. . . .

PERSONAL ESSAY

1   I am a nineteen-year-old Taiwanese woman. My education began when I was seven years old. After studying in Taiwan for nine years, I immigrated to Singapore with my family in December 1981 and continued my studies in Secondary School. I graduated after one year and

5   was accepted to Hwa Chong Junior College, which is one of the best junior colleges in Singapore.

All the courses I studied in Singapore were science subjects based on the syllabus of the Singapore-Cambridge General Certificate of Education. In December 1982, I took the G.C.E. "O" Level Examina-

10   tion. In December 1984, I also took the "A" Level Examination. During
      those three years in Singapore, my English improved greatly as all the
      courses were taught in English.
           While a student in Singapore, I participated in many extracur-
      ricular activities. In Secondary School I was president of the Physics
15   Society and a member of the Mathematics Society. I also participated in
      the National Students Translation Competition and the All School Stu-
      dents Bilingual Essay-Writing Contest. At Hwa Chong Junior College I
      participated in the Courtesy Campaign Essay-Writing competition. I was
      also a member of the Guitar Club and the Badminton Club.
20   Since elementary school, my favorite subject has always been
      mathematics. I am also interested in computer programming and my
      proposed major is Computer Science. I am especially interested in com-
      puter applications in business and in Management Science.

Exercise A   *The University of California suggests some possible topics to its applicants. Which of the following topics does the Taiwanese woman write about? What information does she give?*

			yes/no	information
Ex:	1.	community service	no	_____
	2.	awards	____	_____
	3.	class offices	____	_____
Ex:	4.	school activities	yes	Physics Society
	5.	work experience	____	_____
	6.	educational and career goals	____	_____

Exercise B   *Answer the following questions concerning the organization of the model essay.*

1. In which paragraph does the writer mention her family background?
2. In which paragraph does she mention which schools she has attended?
3. What is the second paragraph about? How is the information in the second paragraph different from the information in the first paragraph?
4. Which of the suggested topics does the third paragraph deal with?
5. What is the topic of the last paragraph?

Practice 2. Purpose and Relevance

You may not know exactly what you are going to say in an essay before you begin writing, but you should have a very clear idea of what your purpose is, of what you are trying to accomplish. Is your purpose to convince the reader of something, to explain how something works, or to interpret the meaning of a situation? Is your purpose to report the results of a laboratory experiment or to show a teacher that you have understood the content of a course?

When you know exactly what you are trying to do, you will be able to decide which information is relevant, or useful. Do not include any information which will not help you achieve your purpose. The Taiwanese woman, for example, may have been greatly influenced by her grandfather, but she does not mention him in her essay because this aspect of her life is not relevant to a university application. It would not help her be accepted to a university.

Note: If you have directions to follow, study them carefully before beginning to write. The directions will indicate what your purpose should be.

Exercise A   *Which of the following **best** states the purpose of the model essay?*

1. to show that the writer is a pleasant young woman
2. to show that she is active in student affairs
3. to show that she is a serious student with broad interests
4. to give the most important facts in her life
5. to show how well she can write English
6. to explain the educational system in Singapore

Exercise B   *Which of the following would not help the writer achieve her purpose? Which would not be relevant to a university application? If you disagree with your classmates, explain why you think something is or is not relevant.*

Ex: 1. her boyfriend—not relevant
2. a prize in a photography contest
3. other members of her family
4. foreign travel
5. hobbies and recreation
6. her family's social position
7. work in her school library
8. her impressions of America
9. her favorite kind of movie
10. her reasons for wanting to go to the University of California
11. her political opinions

Exercise C   *In the following paragraphs, is there any information which is not relevant or necessary? The paragraphs are from essays applying to a university or applying for a job.*

Ex: 1. I have been working as a clerk for two years at an import/export company. Before that, I worked for three years in the accounting department of a construction company. My typing was not very good so I took a typing course in the evenings. I type forty words per minute. I would like to become a clerk in your office. I would work very hard. I hope I will hear from you soon.

2. My name is Masetoshi Park. I am nineteen years old. I have lived in Japan since I was born, but my nationality is Korean. That is why I cannot speak Korean as well as Japanese. After nine years of elementary education, I was admitted to Kamakura Gakuen Senior High School, a very good private school for males. I studied English in high school and when I graduated I took TOEFL and got a score of 470. Now I would like to continue my studies in the United States.

3. I was born in Palau in Micronesia and lived there for sixteen years. It is a lagoon island about 199 miles square. On the island, I spent most of my time with my parents. We depend on the ocean for food. After elementary school, I went to Palau High school. I immigrated to the United States after two years and finished high school in Los Angeles. Now I would like to apply to your university.

Practice 3. Keeping the Reader in Mind

It is important to make your writing fit your reader. In the model essay you may not have understood what a "G.C.E. 'O' Level Examination" is. If the Taiwanese woman had been writing the essay for you, she would have explained these terms. She did not explain them, however, because she realized that her reader, a university admissions officer, would be familiar with these exams in the British educational system. Keep in mind what your reader knows and does not know; explain anything that may be unclear.

Exercise A *Which of the following information would be new to you? To a university admissions officer? Mark the blanks "new" or "old."*

		You	Admissions Officer
Ex:	1. The capital of Taiwan is Taipei.		old
	2. I went to elementary school in Taipei.	new	
	3. I went to elementary school before high school.		
	4. Education in Singapore is based on the British system.		
	5. Hwa Chong Junior College is one of the best in Singapore.		
	6. In high school I was in the Physics Society.		
	7. Computers are important in business.		
	8. My proposed major is Computer Science.		

Exercise B *For whom would the following be new? Old?*

	ESL teacher	American student	Your father
1. TOEFL test			
2. capital of Indonesia			
3. silicon chip			

4. modal auxiliary
5. Ramadan
6. the Fourth of July
7. the national dish of Korea
8. social problems in your country

CYCLE TWO

Practice 4. Organizing Information Into Paragraphs

Essays are made up of paragraphs. Learning how to group information into paragraphs is very important.

To begin writing good paragraphs, you should concern yourself with two problems: logic and quantity. The information in a paragraph must be logically connected in some way; and most of the paragraphs you will write in this course should have at least four or five sentences.

This problem can best be understood by considering some examples. A person who was involved in only one extracurricular activity in high school would probably not write a whole paragraph about extracurricular activities: There is not enough to say about this topic. But this information might logically be included in a paragraph about education or a paragraph about special interests. To give another example, a person who has had only one job might not be able to write a whole paragraph about work experience. This information might, however, fit into a paragraph about special skills, if some skill was learned on the job, or into a paragraph about future goals, if the job experience influenced the person's choice of career.

Remember, though, to be logical. It would make no sense to combine information about a job and a favorite sport in one paragraph: There is no meaningful connection between these bits of information.

Exercise   *Following are notes that two students made when preparing to write personal essays. The first student was writing a university application, the second a job application. Neither of them had enough information to write a good paragraph on each topic. How would you organize this information if you wanted to write an essay of three or four paragraphs?*

A

General Background:	Indonesian, Jakarta, 18 years old.
Education:	Graduated high school 1985, natural science.
	One semester Univ. of San Francisco: ESL.
	Certificate Royal School of Music (London)
Work:	Taught children piano after school
Activities:	School orchestra
Awards:	School piano festival award
Special Skills:	Bilingual: Chinese, Indonesian
Goals and Interests:	Physics, business. Major: Business Admin.

B

General Background:	Colombian, 24 years old; in U.S. for 6 years
Education:	B.A. 1984, Univ. of Texas, Austin: Business Admin.
Work:	Summer job in insurance company, Houston, 1983 (student internship); worked for company importing farm machinery, Bogotá, 1979–80
Activities:	Honor Society, Univ. of Texas
Awards:	B.A. with honors
Special Skills:	Experience with computers, especially billing, Houston, 1983 Worked in accounting, Bogotá, 1979–80. Bilingual: Spanish, English
Goals:	Work for American company doing business with Latin America; interested in sales, import/export

Practice 5. Directed Writing: An Application

Write a personal essay applying to a university or for a job. Take notes before you begin writing. The topics that follow might help you get started. When you have written down as much information as you can think of, decide, first, which information you want to use (which information is relevant) and then how to group the information into paragraphs. Your essay will probably have three or four paragraphs.

Be sure to keep your purpose clearly in mind. The emphasis in an essay applying for a job is obviously a bit different from the emphasis in an essay applying to a university. Also, if you decide to apply for a job, decide before you begin exactly what kind of job you are applying for.

Notes:

Background:

Education:

Work:

Volunteer Work:

Clubs or Activities:

Awards:

Special Skills:

Interests, Hobbies:

Goals:

ADDING ON

Practice 6. Organizing by Time

One of the basic methods of organizing information is by time. In writing about educational experience or work history, you may have begun with the earliest and finished with the most recent, or done just the opposite. You can make such organization clear to the reader by using *time signals:* words or phrases that make the time sequence obvious. In the following paragraph, notice that the writer has placed most of the time signals at the beginning of the sentences, where they will stand out clearly:

> I completed my elementary and high school education in Lebanon and I graduated from the City College of San Francisco *in 1980* with a degree in Hotel and Restaurant Management. *In 1981,* I completed the course in Food Preparation at the College of San Mateo with highest honors. *After finishing this course,* I started to work for the Hyatt Corporation. *In August 1983,* I was nominated the Employee of the Year of the Hyatt Regency Hotel in San Francisco. As a result of that, I was promoted from the position of Food Server to the position of Dining Room Manager. *Two years later* I was made Banquet Manager of the Hyatt Del Monte of Monterey, California.

Exercise *Use the following time information to fill in the blanks in the paragraph which follows. Try to express the time relations in a variety of ways: Do not write "In 19■■" in every sentence.*

Time Sequence

1970–76	Elementary education, People's Republic of China
1976	Immigrated to Hong Kong
1977	Began secondary education
1980	Took Hong Kong Certificate of Education Examination
1980	Took General Certificate of Education "O" Level Exam
1982	Took G.C.E. "A" Level Exam
1985	Came to U.S. Studied ESL at The American Language Institute, Columbia University, for six months
1986	Began Hunter College, New York

Ex: 1 I completed my elementary education in Mainland China. __In 1976__,
2 I immigrated to Hong Kong with my family. _____, I began my
3 secondary education, concentrating on science. _____, I took the

4   Hong Kong Certificate of Education Exam. _____, I also took the
5   G.C.E. "O" Level exam and _____ I took the G.C.E. "A" Level
6   exam. _____, I came to the United States and enrolled in the
     American Language Institute at Columbia University, where I studied ESL
7,8 _____. _____, I began studying at Hunter College in
     New York City.

Practice 7. Adjective Clauses

To develop an advanced writing style, it is very important to be able to use adjective clauses easily and correctly. Using adjective clauses, you can combine several ideas, or bits of information, into a single sentence:

   a.   I worked for a <u>company</u>. <u>It</u> imports <u>farm machinery</u>. We market <u>the</u> <u>farm</u> <u>machinery</u> in several South American countries.

   b.   I worked for a company <u>that</u> imports farm machinery <u>which</u> we market in several South American countries.

As you can see from these examples, it is possible to use an adjective clause when a word, phrase, or idea is *repeated.* In the first example the pronoun *it* is a repetition of the word *company,* and the words *farm machinery* are repeated. In this example, the repeated words—*it* and *farm machinery*—are replaced by *that* and *which.* Words used in this way—*which, who, that,* and so on—may be called *combining pronouns:* They replace a repeated word and combine two or more sentences into one.

Structures like *that imports farm machinery* are sometimes called *adjective clauses:* Like adjectives, they give information about a noun, and like all clauses, they contain at least a subject and a verb:

   c.   I worked for a <u>company</u>   <u>that</u>   <u>imports</u> farm machinery.
              noun   subject verb

In the preceding example, the combining pronoun <u>that</u> is functioning as the subject of the clause. In the next example <u>that</u> is functioning as the object of the adjective clause:

   d.   The farm machinery was in great demand. I sold <u>it</u>.

        The farm machinery <u>that</u> <u>I</u> <u>sold</u> was in great demand.
                     object s   vb

Notice also that a combining pronoun functioning as an object can often be removed:

   e.   The farm machinery   <u>I sold</u> was in great demand.

There are a number of common problems to watch out for in using adjective clauses. (In this book the symbol * indicates that a sentence is incorrect.) First, an adjective clause should be placed right after the noun it refers to:

    f.   *The <u>farm</u> <u>machinery</u> was in great demand <u>that</u> I <u>sold</u>.

The writer sold machinery, not "demand." You can also see from this example that it is sometimes necessary to open up a sentence so that an adjective clause can be placed right after the noun it refers to:

    g. <u>The farm machinery</u> ADJECTIVE CLAUSE <u>was in great demand</u>.

original sentence

Be careful also to use the correct combining pronoun: The combining pronoun *who* refers to persons; *which* refers to anything that is not a person; *that* may refer to either. Avoid errors such as:

    h.   *The company who I worked for was German.

Also, when using adjective clauses, be sure to write complete sentences. An adjective clause cannot stand alone:

    i.   I worked for a company.* Which was German.

The following is another type of incomplete sentence:

    j.   *The <u>company</u> that <u>I</u> <u>worked</u> for.
                s   s   v

A sentence containing an adjective clause must contain at least two subjects and two verbs. The preceding example is incomplete because there is no verb for the first subject, "company."

       On the other hand, be careful not to add unnecessary subjects or objects:

    k.   *The containers <u>that</u> we manufactured <u>them</u> were high quality.
                obj.   obj.

    l.   *The man <u>who</u> <u>he</u> hired me is named Mr. Holmes.
              s   s·

In example k, the object of the adjective clause is unnecessarily repeated; in example l, the subject is repeated.

Exercise A   *Some of the following sentences are incorrect and some are correct. Decide which ones contain errors and correct them.*

Ex: 1. The high school that I went to emphasizes science. (No error.)

Ex: 2. The courses gave me the most trouble were physics and calculus. (Incomplete: The courses <u>that</u> gave me the most trouble were physics and calculus.)

      3. The company that I worked for it made women's clothing.

      4. I took some science courses. That were taught in English.

      5. In the summers I worked for a friend's company who imports and exports agricultural products.

6. I was a member of a volunteer program which tries to raise money for scholarships.
7. After graduating from high school, I worked for an uncle who he has a wholesale business.
8. The teacher told me about your program in Management Science who convinced me to study abroad.

Exercise B *Use adjective clauses to combine the following pairs of sentences into one sentence, if possible—it will only be possible if the second sentence contains a repetition. When combining, make the second sentence the adjective clause. Do not punctuate the adjective clauses in this exercise with commas.*

Ex: 1. When I graduated, I worked for an import/export company. It has offices in Hong Kong and San Francisco.
When I graduated, I worked for an import/export company that (or which) has offices in Hong Kong and San Francisco.

Ex: 2. Music was my favorite subject in high school. After graduating I gave private lessons for two years.
No repetition.

3. I studied at a business school. It is quite well known in my country.
4. A woman told me that your company is very good to work for. She used to work for you.
5. It is difficult to major in technical fields in my country. I came to the United States because I would like to study DP.
6. I grew up in a small village. It has only about 300 people.
7. The secretary told me you might have an opening in your sales department. I spoke to her on the phone last week.
8. A language institute promised me I could learn English in eight weeks. I went to this school when I first got here.
9. I want to learn technical skills. I can use technical skills to get a job in my country.
10. Developing countries need people with technical backgrounds. I want to study mechanical engineering.
11. An uncle convinced me to study law. I have always admired him.
12. I would like to open a restaurant. It would offer both Chinese and Vietnamese food.

Practice 8. Verb Tense

Verbs can be difficult in a personal essay because the tense will change as the discussion moves from the past to the present.

Past Time Period
If you are discussing a period of your life which is clearly finished (*last year, when I was in high school*), you will use a past tense, most often the simple past tense:

a. When I <u>was</u> in high school, I <u>studied</u> science.

Present Time Period

The choice of verb tense is more complicated, however, if you are discussing a present time period, that is, one which is not finished. Notice, first, that the notion *present time period* must be understood in a very general way. An older person might say

b. <u>In my life</u> I have studied several languages, especially German and Russian. <u>For the last three years</u> I have been studying English. <u>This semester</u> I am also taking French.

This person's life is not finished, studying English is not finished, and this semester is not finished; they are all present time periods.

Notice, however, that in this last example three different verb tenses are used: the present perfect (*have studied*), the present perfect progressive (*have been studying*), and the present progressive (*am taking*). The choice of verb tense in a present time period depends on whether the action described is completed or incomplete, in other words, finished or unfinished. Consider the same sentences again:

c. In my life I <u>have studied</u> several languages, especially German and Russian.

The verb tense in this sentence indicates that this person is no longer studying German and French: Those activities are completed, finished. The verb tense most often used to show that an activity in a present time period is finished is the present perfect (*has* or *have* + the past principle).

If neither the activity nor the time period is finished, the two most common choices are:

d. For the last three years I <u>have been studying</u> English.

e. This semester I <u>am</u> also <u>taking</u> French.

If it is clear *how long* an activity has been in progress, as in example d (*for the last three years*), the tense most often used is the present perfect progressive (*has* or *have* + *been* + the past participle). If it is not indicated how long an activity has been in progress, as in example e, the tense most often used is the present progressive (*am, is,* or *are* + the -ing form of the verb).

Here is a summary of the tenses just discussed:

Time Period	Action	Tense
past	finished	one of the past tenses (example a)
present	finished	present perfect (example c)
present	unfinished	present progressive (example e)
present	unfinished + how long	present perfect progressive (example d)

The preceding explanation is a bit simplified but will cover most of the cases that will occur in a personal essay. Nevertheless, there are two exceptions you should be aware of. First, there are some verbs which usually do not take the progressive tenses even if the situation being described is unfinished:

f. She <u>has</u> a degree in economics.

g. She <u>is</u> an economist.

h. I <u>have known</u> her for five years.

Second, it is often possible to use either the present perfect or the present perfect progressive to express duration (how long); the distinction is not always as neat as the preceding summary may make it seem:

i. He <u>has been living</u> in Houston for several years.

(or) He <u>has lived</u> in Houston for several years.

There is one final point to keep in mind before doing the following exercises: Not every sentence contains a time phrase making the relevant time period obvious. In the following paragraph the first three words indicate that the time period is a present one; these words govern, or control, the entire paragraph:

j. <u>At the moment</u> I am finishing my general requirements. I have already taken American history and the introductory data processing courses. I am also working as a tutor in the data processing lab.

Exercise A *Fill in the blanks in the following paragraphs using the correct tense of the verb given in parentheses.*

Ex: a. 1,2 When I ____was____ (be) in high school, I ____had____ (have) a job
3 working for the government. I _____ (work) as a clerk for the Unemployment Development Department in the summer of 1981. The
4 following summer, I _____ (work) as an activities leader for the Boys' Club of America.
5 For the past two years, I _____ (go) to college full time. My
6,7 major _____ (be) Computer Science. I _____ (complete) most of the courses required for the Associate of Arts Degree. This semester
8 I _____ (take) some of the general education courses required to
9 transfer to the university: composition, art history, and sociology. I _____ (apply) to your university because of its excellent program in computer science.

   b. 1. My favorite subjects have always been drama and film. Since I _____
   2. _____ (be) twelve or thirteen, I _____ (want) to be a director. I
   3,4. _____ (make) several short videotapes and I _____ (direct) two plays. In my junior year of high school, I _____ (direct)
   5. _____ (direct)
   6. *The Glass Menagerie* in English, and in my senior year we _____
   7. (produce) *Waiting for Godot* in Japanese. In high school I _____
   8. (be) also president of the Film Club. Every week we _____ (pre-
   9. sent) a European or an American film. At the moment I _____
   10. (take) courses in film history, acting, and modern American drama. I _____ (plan) to get a B.A. and perhaps an M.A. in film or drama.

Exercise B *Check the verbs in the following essay and correct any errors you find.*

Ex: I completed elementary and high school in Vietnam. I graduate from a
Chinese-Vietnamese high school. While I was in high school, I also take
English courses in the Vietnamese-American Association. In 1974 I get a
good score on an English proficiency examination. After I finish high
school, I also take courses in typing and accounting at a business school.

I have come to the United States in 1982. I lived in San Francisco for
one year before I come to San Jose. In San Francisco I work for a Viet-
namese doctor. I answered the telephone, make appointments, and do the
accounting for the office.

Now I am here for two years. My first year here I work in a grocery
store but then I got a better job. For the past year I am work for an im-
port/export company as an accountant. I like this job very much because I
learn many business procedures, This semester I also take business and
English courses at the community college here.

(above "graduate" is written the correction: graduated*)*

Practice 9. Singular and Plural

Errors in the use of the singular and plural forms of nouns are extremely
common among student writers. The first source of such errors is carelessness.
Most students understand that the noun in the following sentence should be
plural (have an *-s*), but it is very easy to overlook such "small" points while
writing a composition:

    a.   *I have been here for three year.

You can find and correct errors of this kind by taking the time to reread your
compositions carefully.

    Some errors, however, are not so easy to understand:

    b.   *In my country most people do not get a lot of educations.

Words like *education* do not usually have a plural form and are called *noncount*
nouns. It is easy to count years but in most cases impossible to count the idea of
education: It is abstract, formless. This example is probably clear enough, but
many students are understandably confused when told that chairs, for example,
are countable but furniture is not. It is often impossible to decide whether a
noun is count or noncount simply by pointing a finger and trying to count. The
distinction is more complicated than that. There is no one word which captures
the distinction in all cases, but noncount nouns are usually one or more of the
following: indivisible, collective, general, abstract, shapeless. *Water* is not naturally divisible; *rice* is a collection of grains; *furniture* is a general word including
such more specific things as chairs; *education* is abstract; *snow* is shapeless, unlike
a *snowflake,* which is countable. Of course more than one of these words may
describe a single noncount noun: *Water* is indivisible, general, and shapeless.
Here are a few more examples:

Noncount	Count
water	oceans, lakes, raindrops, gallons of water
machinery	cars, tractors, buses
education	schools, courses, classes, teachers
writing	compositions, essays, sentences, paragraphs
chemistry	chemicals, bonds, experiments

The problem is complicated by the fact that many nouns are sometimes count and sometimes noncount depending on their meaning in context:

   c.   Beautiful furniture can be made from wood. (*In general.*)

   d.   Rare wood*s* are expensive. (*Specific kinds of wood.*)

A third cause of error in singular/plural usage is nouns which form the plural in irregular ways: *People, sheep,* and so on do not have an *-s* in the plural. Certain other nouns, on the other hand, have an *-s* in the singular: *physics, economics,* and so forth. Notice also that a count noun used in quantity expressions such as the following is always plural: "one of the student*s*" or "some of the course*s.*"

Exercise   *Correct any errors in singular/plural usage in the following essays.*

Ex: 1.   I am a Moroccan man, twenty-three ~~year~~ years old. I went to one of the best high school in Morocco, where the courses were in both Arabic and French. During the last three year of high school, I studied Automobile Technology.

   After I got my diploma, I was accepted by the Institute of Technologies in Belgium. I studied there for one semester and then went to France to continue studying Automobile Technology. After that I came to the United States and studied English at the University of Miami for almost eight month.

   When I was in Belgium and France, I participated in many extra-curricular activities. In France I was a member of the Foreign Student Club and also the representative of the Moroccan student at the college. In Belgium I played on the Institute's soccer team and won a cup as the best soccer player.

   I have always liked mathematic and science but Automobile Technology is my favorite subject and my proposed major. Please send me informations concerning the Automobile Technology program at your college.

2.   In this essay I would like to talk about one of my best friend. He is a twenty-four-year-old Chinese-Dutch man who has spent most of his life in Jakarta, Indonesia. He is friendly, mature, and an excellent student.

   He has been educated in Indonesia and Holland. He finished two year of junior high school in Jakarta and then went to Holland to continue his study. He finished high school there and then returned to Indonesia, where he is now attending university. He is interested in all science course, but he is an excellent mathematic student and is majoring in architecture.

He is so good in mathematics and sciences that he has taught three or four course. First, in junior high school he gave a mathematics course; during his junior year at the university he got some experiences as an assistant to the mathematic teacher. He is also teaching a courses in mathematics and physics at a high school in Jakarta. Finally, he has won honor in most of his high school and university courses. His grade are always very high.

I think he is the smartest person I know and I am proud to be his friend.

ADDITIONAL WRITING TOPICS

1. Write an essay of three or four paragraphs about a member of your family or a friend. Organize your essay around a few general topics such as this person's special qualities or skills, interests, work experience, or education.
2. Write an essay of three or four paragraphs about an important person in your country. It can be someone you admire or dislike, someone alive or dead. Do not try to give this person's complete life history. Concentrate on why this person is important and organize your essay around a few general topics.
3. Imagine you are a teacher or an employer writing a letter of recommendation for one of your students or for one of the people who works for you. Write a letter of two or three paragraphs discussing this person's special skills and strengths. (Decide exactly what you are recommending this person for so you will know what information is relevant.)
4. Imagine you are a supervisor in a school, store, or business. Write an evaluation report on one of the people who works for you. What are this person's strengths and weaknesses?
5. Write an essay applying to be a summer intern in a field of work that would interest you. (Internships are temporary positions given to students so they can gain practical experience in their field of study. A business student, for example, might be allowed to work for a corporation for a summer.)
6. Imagine that you are a businessperson writing a letter to apply for a permit to open a business in the city of your choice. What is your business experience? Why would the business you want to open be good for the community?
7. Imagine you are a graduate student or a researcher. Write a letter applying for a grant (money) to do research on a topic in your area of specialization. What are your qualifications and experience? Why is your research project important?

Lesson 2

TELLING AND INTERPRETING STORIES

Subject: Fairy Tales, Myths, and Fables

Contents:

INTRODUCTION

To be an effective writer, you must be able to convince your reader that your ideas are reasonable, valid, or true. To do this you must support your ideas. In this lesson you will practice supporting general ideas with specific examples.

In Cycle One you will study an essay on the topic of fairy tales to see how general ideas and specific examples are mixed together. You will then practice making generalizations and supporting them in a number of exercises. You will see that a paragraph often consists of one general idea which is supported with a variety of specific examples. The sentence expressing the most general idea of such a paragraph is often called the *topic sentence*.

In Cycle Two you will write an essay interpreting the fairy tale "Cinderella." Before writing you will practice gathering and organizing information (as you did in Lesson 1). The essay that you write will consist of generalizations (expressed in topic sentences) and support (specific examples from the story).

The third section of the lesson, Adding On, introduces additional organizational and grammatical patterns which will be useful when you write your final essay in this lesson.

CYCLE ONE

Practice 1. Reading

ARE FAIRY TALES GOOD FOR CHILDREN?

1

Some of the best known fairy tales have existed for hundreds of years. To have remained popular for so long they must have a very powerful influence on the imaginations of both children and adults.

5

However, many modern parents feel uncomfortable telling certain fairy tales to their children because they feel they are too cruel and frightening. Parents may also feel that some of the ideas or values taught in fairy tales are not appropriate for young children.

The problem can be seen by looking at a story such as "Hansel and Gretel." In this story a cruel stepmother convinces her weak husband

10

that they should abandon their children in the forest and leave them to die because they are so poor there is not enough for them all to eat. Against his wishes, the father takes his young children, Hansel and Gretel, into the forest and leaves them.

15

Alone, frightened, and hungry, the children wander about the forest until they discover a wonderful house made of gingerbread. They immediately begin to eat parts of the house. While they are eating, an old woman comes out and asks them to come into the house. As she seems friendly, the children gladly enter, but the old woman turns out to be a wicked witch. She puts Hansel in a cage and tries to fatten him so

20

that she can eat him.

The woman comes to visit Hansel every day to see if he is fat enough, but he is able to fool the nearsighted old woman by sticking a bone, instead of his finger, out of the cage for her to feel. One day Gretel is able to trick the witch and throw her into the oven. The witch is killed
25 and the children manage to find their way home, taking with them the witch's jewels and money. The wicked stepmother dies and the father and the two children live happily ever after.

To many readers this story seems terribly cruel and violent. What could be more cruel than parents who would abandon their chil-
30 dren in a forest? When the children are captured by the wicked old witch, the story introduces the idea of cannibalism, the possibility that the children will be eaten by the old witch. This idea is made especially dramatic and frightening by the woman's daily visit to Hansel's cage. The story's climax is equally cruel: Gretel burns the witch alive. Such
35 violence and cruelty might create unhealthy fears in a young child.

Violence and cruelty, however, are not the only things people might question in fairy tales. Some people object to the way fairy tales usually present family and sex roles. For example, in "Hansel and Gretel," as in many fairy tales, women are shown to be cruel and destruc-

40 tive. Fairy tales are full of mean stepmothers and wicked witches—mean and wicked women. In fairy tales women and girls are supposed to be weak and passive. The stepmother in "Hansel and Gretel" is bad not only because she is mean to the children but also because she controls her weak husband, because she goes beyond the role of a proper wife.
45 Also, until the end of the story, Hansel leads and Gretel follows. Some parents object to children learning such traditional values.

However, some parents—and psychologists—say that we are missing the point to fairy tales if we worry that children will be frightened or negatively influenced by them. The psychologist Bruno Bet-
50 telheim points out that all children fear being separated from their parents or even abandoned by them (1976, 15–16). This fear is not taught by the story: All children carry it within themselves. According to Bettelheim, "Hansel and Gretel" actually reassures children because it teaches them that they can survive separation from their parents. It
55 teaches children that they can learn to take care of themselves. Hansel and Gretel are both able to trick the witch, survive, and find their way home. Bettelheim also points out that the little girl is no longer passive by the end of the story. She saves her brother and helps discover the way home. Fairy tales teach that fears and problems can be conquered: They
60 always end happily.

Reference

Bettelheim, Bruno. 1976. *The Uses of Enchantment: The Meaning and Uses of Fairy Tales.* New York: Knopf.

Questions

1. Why do some people object to fairy tales?
2. Why are Hansel and Gretel left in the forest?
3. How does Hansel trick the witch?
4. What are some examples of cruelty in this story?
5. What are the stereotyped family roles in this story?
6. According to Bettelheim, why do children like this story?

Practice 2. General and Specific: Exemplification

Many people have not read a fairy tale since they were children. To them it might not be obvious that "fairy tales are cruel and violent." Without examples to support it, this general idea is not convincing or even interesting. But most people would accept the idea if it were supported as follows:

General: Fairy tales are cruel and violent.

Specific: The children are abandoned by their parents.
The witch is going to eat the children.
The girl burns the witch alive.

These three specific details from the story are examples of cruelty and violence. They support the general idea.

Exercise A   *"Fairy tales are cruel and violent" is not the only generalization in the reading. And the previous examples are not the only specifics. Answer the following questions which refer to the use of generalization and examples in the reading.*

1. Paragraph 6 (lines 36–46) of the introductory reading says some people object to the way family and sex roles are presented in fairy tales. What examples support this generalization?

2. In paragraph 7 (lines 47–60), what general idea does this example support: "Hansel and Gretel are both able to trick the witch, survive, and find their way home"?

3. In paragraph 7, what general idea does this example support: ". . . she saves her brother and helps discover the way home"?

Exercise B   *In each group of sentences, one sentence is more general than the others. Decide which one it is.*

Ex: 1.   _____Gretel burns the witch alive.

   ___G___Fairy tales are often cruel and violent.

   _____The children are abandoned by their parents.

   _____The witch is going to eat the children.

2.   _____Fairy tales often deal with a family conflict.

   _____Cinderella is treated very unfairly by her stepmother and stepsisters.

   _____The wicked stepmother forces Hansel and Gretel's father to abandon them in the forest.

   _____In "Snow White" the wicked stepmother is jealous of her beautiful stepdaughter.

3.   _____At the end of the story Cinderella wins out over her wicked stepsisters.

   _____Young Gretel pushes the wicked witch into the oven.

   _____Snow White marries the Prince and her stepmother dies.

   _____In fairy tales, the innocent conquer the wicked.

4.   _____The tortoise wins the race with the rabbit because he never gives up.

   _____Fables, or stories about animals, teach moral lessons.

   _____In a fable called "The Ant and the Grasshopper" the grasshopper is faced with starvation because he has spent the summer singing and dancing instead of growing food for the winter like the ant.

   _____Another fable teaches the danger of vanity: One day a fox sees a crow on a branch with a piece of cheese in his mouth. The fox tells the crow that he has a beautiful voice and asks him to sing a song; the crow cannot resist the compliment and begins to sing, letting the cheese fall to the ground where the fox snaps it up.

Practice 3. Topic Sentences

One common type of paragraph presents and develops one general idea. The sentence which expresses this general idea is usually called the *topic sentence* because it states the subject, or the topic, that the paragraph will develop. The topic sentence is often at or near the beginning of the paragraph although this is not always the case.

Examples of topic sentences can be seen in the introductory reading. The clearest examples are in paragraph 5 (line 28) ("To many readers this story seems terribly cruel and violent") and paragraph 6 (lines 37–38) ("Some people object to the way fairy tales usually present family and sex roles"). The other sentences in the paragraphs support these generalizations with examples.

In a paragraph of this type, all the information must be directly and clearly related to the topic idea. All the information must be relevant. If the topic of the paragraph is the idea of cruelty, it would not be relevant to discuss how Hansel tricks the witch. Trickery would be another topic.

Sometimes in the process of writing, a general idea will occur to you and you will then look for specifics to support it. At other times, examples will occur to you before the general idea that will tie them together. The topic sentence, or general idea, that you finally choose should be general enough to cover all the information you wish to include but not more general than necessary. In the following paragraph, for example, a topic sentence containing the key word *jealousy* would be appropriate because all the examples have to do with the subject of jealousy.

a. <u>In many fairy tales important characters are motivated by jealousy.</u> Cinderella's sisters make her stay home because they are jealous of her beauty and goodness of character. In "Snow White" the stepmother hires someone to kill the girl because one day her mirror tells her that Snow White is a thousand times more beautiful than she is. She is envious of the girl's youth and growing beauty.

Neither of these topic sentences would be appropriate:

b. Important characters may be motivated by <u>evil.</u>

c. The evil characters are sometimes <u>older women jealous of younger ones.</u>

The word *evil* is much more general than necessary; the idea that older women may be jealous of younger women is too specific for the some of information in this paragraph: Cinderella's sisters are not much older than she is.

In the following paragraph, however, the very general word *evil* would be appropriate because the examples are quite varied; a word such as *jealousy* would be too specific:

d. <u>In fairy tales the innocent conquer the evil.</u> Young Gretel pushes the wicked witch into her own oven. At the end of "Cinderella" the innocent young girl wins out over her wicked stepsisters. Snow White marries the Prince, and the evil stepmother dies.

In summary, be sure that your topic sentences fit the information you wish to discuss, or to put it a different way, be sure the information you wish to discuss fits the topic sentence you have chosen.

Exercise A   *Consider the specific examples in each paragraph and write a good topic sentence—one that is neither too general nor too specific—for each one.*

Ex: 1.   _____

_____. The tortoise wins the race against the hare because he never stops to rest. He is slow but determined. In the "Ant and the Grasshopper" the hard-working ant refuses to help the fun-loving grasshopper. The grasshopper has been singing and dancing all summer instead of working; now that winter is approaching he faces starvation.

Possible Topic Sentences
Fables sometimes teach that hard work is the greatest virtue.
Fables sometimes warn us to think ahead.
In fables laziness is often punished.

2.   _____

_____. Hansel survives by fooling the witch: by sticking a bone out of his cage every day, he tricks her into thinking that he is not fat enough to eat. Gretel also uses her wits. One day while she is heating up the oven, the witch asks Gretel to climb in and see if it is warm yet. Gretel suspects that the witch is going to close the door behind her so she tells the witch she does not know how to get in. The witch cries, "You stupid goose! Look, I'll show you how." When the witch climbs into the oven, Gretel closes the door on her. To give one more example, in the story of the "Three Little Pigs" only the cleverest pig survives. He tricks the wolf by heating a huge pot of water in his fireplace so that the wolf is boiled alive when he tries to get into the house by coming down the chimney.

3.   "Cinderella" is the best-known fairy tale in the world._____

_____. The best known version—the one with the glass slipper and the pumpkin—is the one written down by a Frenchman, Charles Perrault, at the end of the seventeenth century. However, the story was known in various forms all over Europe much earlier than this. To give one example, it is known that a Scottish version of the story, "Raschin Coatie," dates back to at least 1540. But the story can be traced back much earlier. The story was first written down in China in the ninth century A.D. Indeed, one of the most important elements in the story can be traced back two thousands years to an Egyptian story. In this story, an eagle steals a woman's sandal, flies away with it, and drops it near the pharoah, who is so fascinated by the sandal that he has the entire kingdom searched for the woman who can wear it.

4.   Most of us know only one version of a fairy tale, usually one which was written down rather recently, such as the Perrault version of "Cinderella."

_____. The Perrault version, for example, is the only one which mentions a glass slipper; in other versions of the story the slipper is made of cloth or fur. In the version most of us are familiar with, Cinderella is aided by a fairy godmother. In other versions, the young girl has a pet (a fish in the earliest Chinese version and a calf in the Scottish version) which the stepmother kills and eats. In these versions, the young girl is helped by the spirits of the dead animals rather than by a fairy godmother. To give another example, in many versions of the story Cinderella's stepsisters want to marry the Prince so badly that they cut off their toes to make their feet fit into the slipper. In the Perrault version, however, there is no blood.

5. _____

At the beginning of "Jack and the Beanstalk" Jack appears to be very foolish. On his way to market he trades a cow for some beans that a stranger convinces him are magic. His mother is furious at his stupidity but it turns out that Jack is right: The beans are truly magical. In a sense this is a victory over his mother. He is victorious again later in the story when he kills the terrible giant, who might be considered a symbol of the great power that adults have over children. Children love to see Jack win because at times all children feel foolish, weak, and inadequate compared to adults.

Exercise B   *The following sentences are quite general and could be topic sentences. Choose one of these sentences and then write a paragraph supporting the general idea with specific examples. You may want to work in groups to make it easier to find enough examples—two at least, three if possible. Of course you may take examples from fairy tales from any country.*

1. The importance of obedience is a frequent theme in fairy tales.
2. Jealousy or competition between brothers or sisters is a common situation in fairy tales.
3. Many fairy tales teach the dangers of greed.
4. In fairy tales a young man must often perform impossible tasks in order to marry the woman he loves.
5. Fairy tales almost always end happily.
6. Fairy tales often end in marriage.
7. The evil person in a fairy tale is very often a stepmother.
8. It is very common for the hero of a fairy tale to be aided by magic powers.
9. Wicked witches are common in fairy tales.
10. It is surprising how many fairy tales deal with the threat of being eaten, by an animal or by a wicked person.

CYCLE TWO

Practice 4. Story and Summary

The introductory reading includes a short version—a summary—of "Hansel and Gretel," so that readers will be able to understand the points made about the story. In the following exercises you will first tell a story, then summarize it.

Exercise A   *Working in small groups or as a class, tell the story of "Cinderella," providing as many of the details as you can remember. Who are the characters? How do they behave? Why? What happens? How does Cinderella feel? What do the people, places, and things look like? Be specific. The following key words and phrases will help you remember the story:*

father . . . stepmother . . . stepsisters
attitudes toward Cinderella
Cinderella's appearance . . . her housework
the ball is announced
the stepsisters prepare to go
Cinderella not allowed to go
fairy godmother . . . pumpkin . . . mice . . . clothes
godmother's warning
the ball . . . the Prince . . . dancing
forgets time . . . runs out . . . loses slipper
the search for the wearer of the slipper
the marriage

Exercise B   *Write a one-paragraph summary of the story. Note: The verb tenses may be different in a story and a summary. A story is told in the past tenses; a summary is often given in the present tenses (see the summary of "Hansel and Gretel" in the introductory reading).*

Practice 5. Directed Writing: Interpreting a Fairy Tale

Can "Cinderella" be analyzed or interpreted as "Hansel and Gretel" was? What values, hidden or obvious, is the story teaching? Does the story appeal to any common childhood worries or problems?

The discussion questions which follow will help you get started. You might want to take some notes on a separate piece of paper as you discuss these questions. Can any of this information logically be divided into paragraphs? Are there any general ideas that can bring different bits of information together? You might want to write an essay with three or four parts:

1. *Introduction:* You might have two or three sentences on the idea that we can look at fairy tales in terms of the values they teach and their appeal to children.
2. *Summary:* You might want to include a paragraph of summary here, perhaps the one you wrote in the last exercise, unless your teacher feels the story is so well known that this is not necessary. (It would be necessary for any other story.)
3. *Values:* What does this story teach children, especially girls? Will you need one paragraph or more to deal with this question? Make sure each paragraph has a clear topic sentence.
4. *Appeal:* Why is this story so popular?

In dealing with the values and appeal of the story be sure to support any generalizations you make with specific examples from the story.

Discussion Questions

1. What does "Cinderella" teach about patience and obedience?
2. Would you tell someone who is treated as badly as Cinderella to be patient and obedient? If not, what would you advise her?
3. What does the story teach about vanity and pride?

4. How important is physical beauty in this story?
5. Why does the Prince immediately fall in love with Cinderella?
6. What does this story teach girls who are not beautiful?
7. How is Cinderella rewarded for her sweet character?
8. What is the importance of marriage in this story?
9. At the end of the story Cinderella forgives her stepsisters. Do you remember what she does for them to show her forgiveness?
10. How do we see women treating each other in this story?
11. The Prince is the main male character in the story. How is he shown?
12. This story deals with jealousy and rivalry in a family. Is the story psychologically realistic? Do you think all children sometimes feel these emotions?
13. Do children sometimes feel that they are being rejected, like Cinderella?
14. Do children sometimes feel they are being punished unfairly?
15. Why do you think children are interested in the theme of obedience?
16. What does the story teach children about such common childhood worries?

ADDING ON

Practice 6. Paragraph Bridges

Each paragraph deals with new information: a new idea, a new problem, a new part of a story. But the reader should not have the impression that an essay is jumping from idea to idea or event to event. The connection between paragraphs should be clear. You can make this connection obvious by repeating some of the information from the preceding paragraph at the beginning of the new paragraph. This repetition of "old" information before the introduction of "new" information can be called a *paragraph bridge:* It leads the reader from one paragraph to another.

An example of a paragraph bridge can be seen in the introductory reading. There is a bridge between paragraph 5 (which deals with violence and cruelty) and paragraph 6 (which deals with family values):

Paragraph 5.   To many readers this story seems terribly <u>cruel and violent</u>. What could be more <u>cruel</u> than parents who would abandon their children in a forest? . . .

Paragraph 6.   <u>Violence and cruelty</u>, however, are not the only things people might question in fairy tales. Some people object to the way fairy tales usually present <u>family and sex roles</u>.
new topic

In this example, the second sentence of paragraph 6 introduces the new topic: family and sex roles. The first sentence is a bridge sentence, repeating some old information and leading into the new topic.

In the following example, notice that the bridge is not a complete sentence: It can be a clause, a phrase, or even a single repeated word.

    a. As soon as the stepsisters learned of the Prince's ball, they began to make prepa-rations. They could think and talk of nothing else. <u>They spent hours trying on their dresses and deciding how to arrange their hair.</u> One would say, "I think I'll wear my red velvet gown," and the other would reply, "I think I look best in my blue silk gown, don't you?"

    b. <u>One day while they were admiring themselves in the mirror,</u> Cinderella asked her stepmother if she could go too. Her stepmother just laughed and said, "You! What would you wear? Besides, you have too much work to do here.". . .

In this example, notice that the bridge does not repeat the exact words from the preceding paragraph. But the clause "One day while they were admiring them-selves in the mirror" repeats the main idea: the stepsisters' vanity and excitement.

Exercise A *Fill in the blanks in the following passage from "Hansel and Gretel" with paragraph bridges. The italicized information suggests what you might use as your bridge. The first one is done for you:*

1   Once there was a very poor family consisting of two children, Hansel and Gretel, their father, and their mean stepmother. They were so poor that the stepmother wanted *to get rid of the children by abandoning them in the forest.* That way they would not have to share their food among four people. The
5 father resisted this idea but the stepmother was very determined and he finally gave in.

Ex: So one day *Hansel and Gretel were led into the forest* by their stepmother and father. When they reached the middle of the forest, their father told them to gather wood for a fire. Soon they had a large pile which blazed up
10 when it was lit. The woman said, "Now *lie down by the fire* while we go out and cut more wood. When we have finished we will come back and get you."
    So_____
but it got darker and darker, colder and colder, and no one came back to get them. They spent the night alone in the forest, frightened and alone. The
15 next day they wandered about the forest getting hungrier and hungrier. At one point they began to follow a beautiful white bird which led them to a wonderful house made of gingerbread. Hansel said, "We will have a good meal. I will eat a piece of the roof, Gretel, and you can have a piece of the window." He tore off a corner of the roof and part of the window, and the
20 *children began their delicious meal.*
    While _____
they heard a gentle voice call out:

        Nibbling, nibbling like a mouse,
        Who's nibbling at my little house?

25   Then the door opened and an old, old woman came out supporting herself on a cane. At first the children were so frightened that they dropped what they were eating, but the woman calmed them down in a kind voice, saying, "Come in and stay with me. You will not be hurt."

Exercise B *The following essay about a traditional Laotian story is more analytical. Add paragraph bridges which refer back to the main idea of the preceding paragraph. The second paragraph, for example, deals with the most obvious moral of the story. Your paragraph bridge at the beginning of the third paragraph should refer back to this moral.*

HALF A BLANKET

1
    When I was a child I was fascinated by an old Laotian story that my grandmother used to tell me. This story is about three generations living together: a man and wife, their infant son, and the man's old father. The man loves his father but his wife tells him lies about the old man, hoping to

5
get rid of him. Eventually the man is turned against his father and tells him he will have to move out of their house. He builds a little cottage for his father to live in and forgets about him. As time passes, the boy becomes friendly with the old man, although he does not know he is his grandfather. One day the old man asks the boy to bring him a blanket because he is cold

10
in winter. The boy goes home and asks his father, who tells him to go upstairs and get one. The boy comes down with a blanket he has cut in half. When his father asks him why he has cut the blanket in half, he says, "This half is for you when you get old, Father."

    The moral of this story is clear: We must respect and take care of our

15
parents. The husband has forgotten what he owes his father. He has forgotten that he too will grow old. The boy reminds his father of this truth in a very dramatic way. As a child I naturally felt very sorry for the old man, and I was always happy at the end of the story because I knew that justice would be done. I knew the old man would be invited back.

20
_____

_____.

Perhaps another reason I enjoyed this story so much is that the boy, the child, is the hero. The adults are shown to be mean, foolish, weak, or helpless. The woman is mean; her husband is weak and foolish; the old man

25
is helpless to solve his own problem. He would still be living in his cottage if his clever and generous grandson had not helped him. I probably felt that I would have behaved as wisely as the boy if I had been in the same situation.

_____.

30
Now that I am an adult—and a woman—I am interested in another aspect of the story. Now I see that the story has another message: Men should never let themselves be dominated by women. If they do, they will regret it. The man may be weak and foolish but he is not evil; it is the woman who is evil, who is responsible for the old man's having to leave.

35
    This story teaches respect for elders and it shows children that they are important to the family. But it also has a hidden message: Women should not interfere and men should not listen to women.

Practice 7. Time Signals

The basic logic or organizing principle of a story, or a summary of a story, is time sequence. In the first of the following examples the time sequence is not directly stated; in the second and third examples the sequence is made obvious by the underscored words:

a. The clock struck twelve. Cinderella ran out of the ballroom.

b. <u>As soon as</u> the clock struck twelve, Cinderella ran out of the ballroom.

c. The clock struck twelve. <u>Immediately</u> Cinderella ran out of the ballroom.

Expressions like *as soon as* and *immediately*, which make the logic or organization of a piece of writing clearer, will be called *signal expressions* in this book. This very large group of expressions can be divided into two classes: *combining signals* (such as *as soon as*) and *noncombining signals* (such as *immediately*).

Combining signals like *as soon as* are traditionally called *subordinators*. The most common time subordinators are *before, after, when, as soon as, while, as, until, since.* A clause beginning with a combining signal may not stand alone:

d. *<u>As soon as</u> the clock struck midnight.

Such a clause must be combined with another clause, which it may either precede or follow. Notice the punctuation:

e. <u>As soon as</u> the clock struck twelve, Cinderella ran out of the ballroom.

f. Cinderella ran out of the ballroom <u>as soon as</u> the clock struck twelve.

Usually, when the clause containing a combining expression is in the second position, it is not set off by a comma.

The second group of *signal expressions,* the *noncombining signals,* is quite large. Some of the time expressions which could be considered noncombining signals are *first, then, just then, next, after that, at that moment, afterwards, eventually, finally.*

The noncombining signals are sometimes almost the same in meaning as the combining signals, but grammatically they are different. First, as the name indicates, they do not combine clauses. The most common error with noncombining expressions is the following:

g. *The clock struck twelve, <u>immediately</u> Cinderella ran out of the ballroom.

These two clauses must be separated with a period (.) or semicolon (;), not a comma. A second difference between combining and noncombining expressions is that noncombining expressions do not have to be placed at the beginning of the clause:

h. <u>Immediately</u> Cinderella ran out of the ballroom.

i. Cinderella <u>immediately</u> ran out of the ballroom.

j. Cinderella ran out of the ballroom <u>immediately</u>.

Exercise A *The following exercise is based on a Chinese myth which explains why there is no "Year of the Cat" in the Chinese calendar. The story would sound better, and the logic would be clearer, if time signals were added. The time signals to be added are given in parentheses. Decide which clause to add the time signal to and whether any punctuation is needed.*

THE CAT, THE MOUSE, AND THE CHINESE CALENDAR

The Chinese calendar consists of a long cycle and a short cycle. The short cycle is twelve years long and each of these years is named after an animal. This is how the years got their names.

Ex: 1. The Lord of Heaven wanted to select animals to rep-   (many years ago)
resent the years in the short cycle/he picked a place
and made an announcement to all animals.

<u>Many years ago</u> the Lord of Heaven wanted to select
animals to represent the years in the short cycle<u>.</u> He
picked a place and made an announcement to all animals.

He told the animals there would be a race to determine which animals would be chosen. He named a
far-off place, several days journey away and said the
first twelve to arrive would have years named after
them.

2. The animals heard this/they all got busy planning   (as soon as)
their journeys.

3. The cat and the mouse were great friends so they   (at that time)
decided to travel together/they decided that the mouse
would ride on the cat's back because the cat could
travel much faster.

4. They had only been traveling a short time/they came   (when)
to a river and the cat told the mouse that he did not
know how to swim.

5. The mouse was furious/he heard this because he knew   (when)
they would lose the race if they did not get across the
river quickly.

6. They thought for a moment/the mouse said, "You   (then)
   wait here/I swim across.   (while)

7. I get to the other side/I will send a boat over to get   (when)
   you."

8. However, the mouse got to the other side/he forgot   (as soon as)
   all about the cat and hurried on.

9. The cat saw what was happening/he was in a terrible   (when)
   rage.

10. The cat calmed down/he swore that cats would be the   (eventually)
    enemies of mice for all time.

And to this day, as everyone knows, cats still chase
mice. But in the Chinese calendar every twelfth year is
the Year of the Mouse. There is no Year of the Cat.

Exercise B. *Decide what punctuation, if any, is needed to fill in the blanks in the following Japanese fairy tale. If there is no **combining** time signal, you will have to put in a period (and capitalize the first letter of the next word).*

KINDNESS TO A CRANE

Ex: 1. Once upon a time a poor woodcutter lived in a small village ___._H__ he
   worked very hard but was lonely because his wife had died.

Ex: 2. One day as he was coming home from work ___._ he saw a crane. The
   bird had been caught in a trap and was hurt. He felt pity for the crane so he

3. took it home and treated it _____ a few days later the crane was better, so he
   set it free.
   Some months after this, on a cold, snowy night, a beautiful woman ap-

4. peared at his door _____ she said, "I am trying to get to the next village but
   I am lost. Please let me spend the night here." He let her in because she was

5,6. almost frozen with cold _____ after she warmed up _____ they began to

7. talk _____ soon the man found he was falling in love with the beautiful

8. stranger _____ finally he asked her to stay and live with him and she
   agreed.

One day, after they had been living very happily together for some time
9. _____ the woman asked the woodcutter if he could get her a loom so she
10,11. could weave cloth _____ when he brought the loom home _____ she made
12. him promise never to watch her _____ while she worked. He promised.

Every day she worked in her room weaving cloth which the woodcutter
would sell in the village for a good price. It was the most beautiful cloth
13. anyone had ever seen _____ soon the man's curiosity became too strong for
him to control and he peeked into the room where she was working. He was
amazed to see a crane weaving the beautiful cloth out of its own feathers
14,15. _____ when the crane saw the man watching _____ it wept, saying, "Didn't
you promise? Now that you have seen my real form, I must leave." The
16. crane thanked him for his kindness _____ then all of a sudden the room
17,18. was empty _____ when the man went to the window _____ he saw a
19. beautiful crane flying high in the sky _____ now he was alone again.

Practice 8. Run-on Sentences

One of the most common errors for student writers is called the *run-on sentence*.

    a.   *An old woman lived in the house, she surprised Hansel and Gretel they were eating parts of her home.

In this example, the "sentence" consists of three clauses; that is, there are three subjects (*old woman, she,* and *they*) and three verbs (*lived, surprised,* and *were eating*). Clauses must be either separated by periods or semicolons (*not* commas) or connected with *combining words*. Perhaps the most common combining words are *and, but, so,* and *or.* In this book you have also studied two other types of combining words: combining pronouns such as *who, which,* and *that* (Lesson 1, Practice 7), and in the preceding exercises, combining time signals such as *before, after, when,* and *so on.*

Notice that the easiest solutions are not always the best:

    b.   An old woman lived in the house. She surprised Hansel and Gretel. They were eating parts of her home.

    c.   *An old woman lived in the house and she surprised Hansel and Gretel and they were eating parts of her house.

Before separating everything with periods or combining everything with *and* or *but,* consider whether other combining words might be used:

    d.   The old woman <u>who</u> lived in the house surprised Hansel and Gretel <u>while</u> they were eating parts of her house.

While and *who* make the logic of the sentence clearer than *and* because their meaning is more precise.

Exercise *Correct the run-ons in the following Arabic story. If possible, use combining words; but remember that it is not always possible: Periods are not always bad.*

ALI BABA AND THE THIEVES

Ex: A long time ago there lived a man named Ali Baba, ~~he~~ who was a simple woodcutter.

Ex: One day Ali Baba was in the forest cutting trees_ after awhile he got tired .A so he climbed a tree to rest. He slept in the tree, he was awakened by a noise beneath him. Below him he saw a man, he approached a huge rock on the side of a hill. The man said, "Open Sesame," the rock rolled to one side. The man entered the cave, stayed for awhile and then came out. He said "Close Sesame," the rock rolled back into place and the man left.

Ali Baba waited for awhile. He was sure it was safe, he climbed down, went to the rock and said "Open Sesame." The rock rolled away, he entered the cave excitedly. There he saw many boxes, the boxes were full of diamonds and money. While he was looking at the boxes in amazement he heard a group of men approaching, he hid behind a large box. The men turned out to be thieves, they began talking about robbing a house in the village that night. One of the thieves said he would sneak into the village and put a cross on the door of the house so the other robbers would know which house to go to. The robbers all agreed to this idea, then they left.

Ali Baba hurried back to his village as fast as possible wondering how he could stop the thieves. Then he had an idea: He got some paint and went around the village painting a cross on every door, the thieves would be confused when they arrived. The plan worked. When the thieves arrived they were so confused that the villagers captured them easily. They locked them all up, they ran to the cave where they found enough treasure to make them all rich for the rest of their lives!

Practice 9. The Past Tenses

Whereas the present tenses may be used to summarize a story, the past tenses—the simple past, the past progressive, the past perfects—are used to tell a story.

The simple past is the most frequent past tense. It is used to describe actions which occurred in sequence, one after the other, or which happened at the same time:

a. As soon as Cinderella enter<u>ed</u> the ballroom, the Prince <u>saw</u> her. He ask<u>ed</u> everyone who she <u>was</u>. No one <u>knew</u>.

The past progressive is used to indicate that one action was in progress (was not yet finished) when another action occurred:

b. While Cinderella <u>was</u> danc<u>ing</u>, the clock <u>struck</u> midnight.

In this example, notice that the second action or event (*struck*) is in the simple past.

The past perfect tenses are used to express *how long* an action or condition had lasted at a given moment in the past. Both the simple past perfect and the past perfect progressive are used in this meaning:

c. Finally the day of the ball arrived. The stepsisters <u>had</u> talk<u>ed</u> (or *had been* talk*ing*) of nothing else <u>for weeks</u>.

The simple past perfect can also be used to emphasize that one action is completed when another starts:

d. When her stepsisters <u>had left</u> for the ball, Cinderella <u>sat</u> down and <u>wept</u>.

The use of the past perfect in this sentence makes it clear that the stepsisters were gone *before* Cinderella started crying. It would be possible to use the simple past for all the verbs in this sentence, but the time relations might not be quite as clear:

e. When her stepsisters <u>left</u> for the ball, Cinderella <u>sat</u> down and <u>wept</u>.

Exercise Fill in the blanks in the following passage with the correct past tense form of the verbs in parentheses.

Ex: 1,2. Finally the day of the ball ___arrived___ (arrive). The stepsisters _had_
Ex: 3. _spoken_ (speak) of nothing else for weeks. They _____ (spend)
4. days in front of their mirrors trying on their dresses. They _____
(make) Cinderella fix their hair and iron their dresses. At last they _____
5. _____ (be) ready.
6,7. The coach _____ (come) and the stepsisters _____
8,9. (ride) off. As Cinderella _____ (watch) them leave, she _____
10. _____(begin) to weep softly. While she _____ (cry), her fairy god-
11,12. mother _____ (appear) and _____ (ask) her why she
13,14. _____ (cry). When Cinderella _____ (tell) her every-
15. thing, she _____ (say), "Don't worry; all that can easily be taken care of. Go into the garden and bring me a pumpkin." When Cinderella
16,17. _____ (return), the godmother _____ (touch) the pump-
18. kin with her magic wand. Suddenly it _____ (change) into a mag-
19. nificent carriage. Then she _____ (tell) Cinderella to go find six
20. mice, a rat, and six lizards, which she _____ (touch) with her wand, changing them into six horses, a coachman, and six servants. Finally,

21. with another touch of her wand she _____ (turn) Cinderella's dirty rags into a gorgeous ballgown.
22. Cinderella _____ (be) filled with joy. Her godmother quickly
23. _____ (say), "Now hurry along so you won't miss too much of the
24. ball." As Cinderella _____ (run) out the door, the godmother
25. _____ (call) after her, making her promise to be back by midnight.
26,27. Cinderella _____ (swear) she would leave before the clock _____
28. _____ (strike) twelve. Then she _____ (ride) off, waving out the window.

Practice 10. Direct Quotation

Direct quotation gives the reader someone else's exact words. It is used in quite different kinds of writing. You might want to give the exact words of a character in a fairy tale, for example; or later in the course, you might want to quote directly something you have read. There are a number of things to pay attention to when including a direct quotation in your writing.

A direct quotation is usually introduced by a verb such as *said, asked, begged, suggested,* or *pointed out.* These introductory verbs are usually in the simple past tense, but the verbs in the quotation may be in any tense:

   a. The old man was too old to take care of himself so he begg*ed* his son, "Please *don't* make me leave home. I *will* do everything you and your wife say."

Pay special attention to the conventions of punctuation in direct quotation:

1. Quotation marks (". . .") are used at the beginning and end of the quotation.
2. Final punctuation—the period (.), the question mark (?), the exclamation point (!)—is usually placed inside the closing quotation marks: ". . . say." not ". . . say".
3. The quotation is usually separated from the introductory part of the sentence by a comma: ". . . so he begged his son, "Please . . ."
4. If the quotation itself is a complete sentence, the first word is capitalized: "Please don't make me leave home. . . ."
5. A quotation, like the one in this example, may be more than one sentence in length.

Exercise   *In the following exercise you are told who the speaker is (or who the speakers are) and what is said. Use this information to write sentences including direct quotation. You may want to add more information to your sentences.*

		Speaker(s)	**Quotation**
Ex:	1.	stepsisters	who is that beautiful girl

When Cinderella entered the ballroom, the stepsisters asked each other, "Who is that beautiful girl?"

2. stepmother/Cinderella   scrub the floors/wash the windows/make the beds

3. stepsister/stepsister   which dresses should we wear

4. stepmother/Cinderella   no, you certainly cannot go to the ball

5. godmother/Cinderella   I will change a pumpkin into a carriage

6. Prince/several people   does anyone know who that girl is

7. Cinderella   oh, no/it's midnight/I have to go

8. Prince/messengers   find the wearer of this glass slipper

9. messenger   it fits

Practice 11. Indirect Speech

At times you may wish to repeat an idea without using direct quotation, that is, without giving the speaker's exact words. In such cases you may use indirect speech, which differs from direct quotation in a number of ways. Perhaps these differences can best be understood by considering statements first, and then questions.

Statement

In a statement it is often necessary to change pronouns and verb tense:

    a. Cinderella said, "I am scrubbing the floor."
       Cinderella said (that) she was scrubbing the floor.

As in this example, if the verb of introduction is in the past tense (*said*), present tense verbs will change to past tenses.

Quotation	**Indirect Speech**
b. "I wash the clothes."	She <u>said</u> (that) she wash<u>ed</u> the clothes.
c. "I am cleaning."	She said she <u>was</u> cleaning.
d. "I have already dusted."	She said she <u>had</u> already dusted.
e. "I have been working hard."	She said she <u>had</u> been working hard.

Certain modal auxiliaries also change form in indirect speech.

f.   "You <u>can't</u> go."   Her stepmother said she <u>could not</u> go.

These changes can be summarized as follows:

```
can ——————— could
may——————— might
will ——————— would
must
have to——— had to
```

Question

To change a question from direct quotation to indirect speech it may be necessary to make the same changes in pronouns, verb tense, or modal auxiliary. It will also be necessary to make other changes. First, statement, not question, word order is used:

g.   Her stepmother asked, "What <u>could you</u> wear to a ball?"
Her stepmother asked what <u>she could</u> wear to a ball.

Second, the question-forming auxiliaries *do, does,* and *did* are not used in indirect questions:

h.   Her stepsisters asked, "What <u>do you know</u> about good society?"
Her stepsisters asked what <u>she knew</u> about good society.

Third, yes/no questions are introduced by *if* or *whether*:

i.   The Prince inquired, "<u>Does</u> anyone <u>know</u> that girl?"
The Prince inquired <u>if</u> anyone <u>knew</u> the girl.

Notice, finally, that the final punctuation in an indirect question is a period rather than a question mark.

One last point: The important thing in indirect speech is to capture the meaning of the original, not necessarily to use every word in the original. Many spoken expressions do not fit into indirect speech, which is more formal. Sometimes, however, the emotion of a spoken expression can be communicated by the verb of introduction:

j.   The fairy godmother said, "<u>Now listen Cinderella</u>, you have to be back by midnight!"
The fairy godmother <u>warned</u> Cinderella that she had to be back by midnight.

Exercise   *Write sentences based on the following information. Use indirect speech. You will need to add words to write a proper introduction.*

	Speaker(s)	**Quotation**

Ex: 1. stepsister/stepsister   "How does this dress look on me?"

<u>One stepsister asked the other how the dress looked on her.</u>

2. Cinderella/godmother   "I can't go in the clothes I am wearing."

3. Prince/Cinderella   "May I have the next dance?"

4. stepsisters/each other   "Who is the beautiful girl dancing with the Prince?"

5. Cinderella   "Oh, no! It's midnight! I have to go!"

6. Prince/messenger   "Have you found the wearer of the glass slipper yet?"

7. messenger   "It fits!"

8. Cinderella/stepsisters   "Will you come live with me in the castle after I am married?"

Practice 12. Articles

It is difficult for many students to decide whether to use the article *a* (or *an*), the article *the*, or no article at all. The rules for article usage are quite complicated and most students would not be able to remember them all. Fortunately, however, there are a few fairly simple rules which will greatly reduce the number of errors you may make. One such rule is this: If a noun has general reference, it is not usually necessary to use an article. In the following example the symbol Ø (nothing) is used to emphasize that no article is required:

    a. ØAnthropologists have begun studying Øfairy tales because they reflect Øways of thinking. ØFairy tales teach, for example, that Øgoodness is rewarded and Øjustice is done.

These sentences do not refer to any specific anthropologist, any specific fairy tale or way of thinking, or any specific kind of goodness or justice: These nouns have general reference; no article is necessary. In this example notice also that the count nouns are plural in form (*anthropologists, ways, fairy tales*); noncount nouns have no plural form (*goodness, justice*).

The rule just given is all you will need to produce correct sentences in the majority of cases. Do not worry, therefore, if you find nouns with general reference preceded by an article:

> b.   Anthropologists have begun studying <u>the</u> fairy tale. <u>A</u> fairy tale reflects <u>a</u> way of thinking.

The rules governing this last example are complicated and would probably confuse you more than help you.

Exercise   *In the following paragraphs, if a noun has general reference, use no article (Ø). Cross out the incorrect choice.*

Ex: a.

1,2,3,4.   ~~The~~/<u>Ø</u> fairy tales often teach ~~the~~/<u>Ø</u> children a/Ø patience, a/Ø obedience and
5,6.   the/Ø respect for elders. But some parents think the/Ø fairy tales may not
7,8.   always be good for the/Ø children. Should all the/Ø girls behave as Cinder-
9,10.   ella does, for example? Does this story teach a/Ø patience or a/Ø passivity?
11,12,13.   "Cinderella" also teaches the/Ø girls and the/Ø boys that the/Ø beauty will be
14,15.   rewarded, that the/Ø beautiful girls are better than the/Ø unattractive girls.
16.   The/Ø messages such as these bother some parents.

b.   1.   In the/Ø story "Little Red Riding Hood" a little girl disobeys her mother and
2.   gets into trouble. One day her mother asks her to take a/Ø basket of food to
her grandmother. Her mother warns her to go directly to her grand-
3,4.   mother's without stopping in the/Ø forest. Unfortunately, the/Ø little girl
5.   does not listen to her mother and stops in the/Ø forest to pick flowers. While
6.   she is doing this, a/Ø wolf comes up and begins talking to her. He learns that
she is going to her grandmother's so he hurries there before her and eats up
her grandmother. When Little Red Riding Hood gets there, he eats her too.
7.   Like many fairy tales, this one teaches the/Ø obedience. Clearly it also
8,9.   teaches the/Ø children not to talk to the/Ø strangers.

c.   1,2,3.   The/Ø fables are another kind of traditional story. The/Ø fables are the/Ø
4,5.   stories in which the characters are the/Ø animals. A/Ø well-known fable is
6,7,8.   "The/Ø Tortoise and the/Ø Hare." In this fable, a/Ø tortoise wins a race
9,10.   against a/Ø hare, showing the importance of the/Ø determination and the
11.   dangers of a/Ø pride.

ADDITIONAL WRITING ASSIGNMENTS

1. Analyze a fairy tale in terms of what it teaches children. Do you agree with the values it is teaching? Provide a brief summary of the story you are interpreting unless it is extremely well known.

2. Write a traditional fairy tale, fable, or myth from your culture with the intention of entertaining, not explaining or interpreting. Try to include both direct quotation and indirect speech.

3. Make up a children's story of your own. At the end you might want to add a paragraph explaining why you think children would like this story or why it would be good for them.

4. Analyze a popular movie or television program the way you have been analyzing fairy tales. Provide a summary of what happens and an analysis of what it teaches us, directly or indirectly.

5. Write an essay on an important moment in the history of your country. What happened? Why was it important? Do not try to write the whole history of your country in a few paragraphs. Note: If you want to refer to what someone said, use indirect speech—most direct quotation would be too informal for an academic topic of this kind.

Lesson 3

DESCRIBING EVENTS

Subject: Holidays and Ceremonies

Contents:

—Reading
—Including Definition
—Example Signals
—Directed Writing: Halloween
—Adjective Clauses: Restrictive and Nonrestrictive
—Articles
—Repeating for Clarity: *This* and *These*
—Restatement Signals
—The Present Tenses
—The Simple Present Passive

INTRODUCTION

This lesson focuses on clarity—on ways to make your meaning clear, or obvious. The importance of defining unclear terms is emphasized and the use of examples to make an idea clear and convincing is also reviewed.

In Cycle One you will read an essay on a Mexican holiday, "The Day of the Dead." Some of the concepts and many of the words in this essay would not be clear to the average reader. You will see how the writer has included definition in the essay to make the meaning clear. You will practice some of the grammatical patterns that can be used to include definition.

In Cycle Two you will write about a somewhat similar American holiday—Halloween. You will review the use of examples, learn some example signals, and define any terms that would not be clear to a non-American reader.

In Adding On you will practice some of the grammar that makes clear the connection between one sentence and another—in other words, the grammar that ties ideas together.

CYCLE ONE

Practice 1. Reading

MEXICO'S DAY OF THE DEAD

1   On November 2 many Mexicans, especially Indians in the countryside, celebrate the "Day of the Dead," when the spirits of the dead are believed to return. We might expect such a holiday to be a time of sadness and even fear, but in fact people look forward to and enjoy this
5   reunion with their dead loved ones. On this day the living remember, pray for, and "feed" the dead.

Preparations for the return of the dead begin some time before November 2. An altar is set up in the main room of the house. It is decorated with fruit, marigolds—the flower of the dead—and special
10   candy in the shape of skulls and skeletons. The *pan de muerto,* a kind of bread decorated with the dead person's name, is also baked and placed on the altar. At the foot of the altar are placed small dishes of the dead person's favorite foods, for example, tamales (a dish made of sweet cornmeal stuffed with meat). During this time of preparation, the mood
15   is lighthearted and the children especially enjoy themselves.

On the evening of November 2, however, the mood becomes more serious and thoughtful. Families walk to the cemetery, lighting the way with candles. The souls of the dead are escorted to the cemetery by masked dancers. There the mood becomes more lively as people eat and
20   pass around bottles of tequila or pulque, alcoholic drinks made from cactus. The living exchange their memories of the dead, sometimes even acting out scenes from the dead person's life. There may be a band, and *alabadas,* traditional Indian funeral songs, may be sung. All night long the church bells ring.

Figure 3–1

25   The events, symbolism, and mood of this holiday indicate that the Mexican Indian has a special way of viewing death, and life. For the Indian the dead are not completely and finally separated from the living. Life is just one phase in the journey of the soul, a journey which continues after death.

Questions
1. What preparations are made for the arrival of the spirits?
2. What do people do on the night of November 2?
3. Why do people enjoy this holiday? Why do you think children enjoy it most of all?
4. What is the topic of paragraph 2? Of paragraph 3?

5. Are there *paragraph bridges* in this essay? (See Lesson 2, Practice 6 for *paragraph bridges.*)
6. What are: marigolds, tamales, pulque, *pan de muerto, alabadas?* Did you know before you read this essay? Are definitions included in the essay?
7. Is there a similar holiday in your country?

Practice 2. Including Definition

In the preceding reading there were probably several words or concepts which would not have been clear to you without explanation or definition. The writer of the essay realized that many readers would not be familiar with these terms and so defined or explained them. There are many ways to do this but two of the most useful are adjective clauses and appositives:

    a. The altar is decorated with marigolds, which are <u>the flower of the dead,</u> fruit, and candy.   *(Adjective clause.)*

    b. The altar is decorated with marigolds,   <u>the flower of the dead,</u> fruit, and candy.   *(Appositive)*

There are a couple of things to notice concerning these structures. First, adjective clauses and appositives used in this way are separated from the rest of the sentence by punctuation, usually commas, as in the preceding examples. However, dashes (—) or parentheses () are sometimes used instead of commas. They provide a stronger break than commas; dashes are also a bit less formal:

    c. For this day the <u>pan de muerto</u>—a kind of bread decorated with the dead person's name—is baked.

    d. People pass around bottles of tequila or pulque (alcoholic drinks made from cactus).

Notice also that in this type of adjective clause it is important to use *who* or *which,* not *that* (a point which is explained more fully later in the lesson.)

    You can also see from these examples that appositives are closely related to adjective clauses: An appositive is an adjective clause with the combining pronoun (*which* in this case) and the verb be (*are* in this case) removed. In the resulting sentence, one noun structure (*marigolds*) is defined by another noun structure (*the flower of the dead*).

Exercise A   *The underlined words in the following passage would not be clear to most American readers. The definitions of these words follow the passage. Rewrite the passage including definitions. Punctuate with commas, dashes, or parentheses.*

A BUDDHIST CEREMONY IN INDONESIA

Ex: 1. Indonesian Buddhists celebrate <u>Waisak,</u> an important religious holiday, on May 25 during the full moon. Waisak celebrates Buddha's birth, his

2. reaching <u>Nirvana,</u> and his death.

Preparations for this large ceremony begin about three weeks before May

3. 25. The site of the ceremony is decorated with *teratai* and *sedap melam*. Tea,

4. rice, and *gulalei* are wrapped and put into paper bags, which will be given to

5. visitors. During this period of preparation, a large quantity of *air jahe* is also made. An altar is set up and decorated with these flowers, foods, and drinks.

Definitions

Ex: 1. <u>Waisak</u> is an important religious holiday.

2. Nirvana is the state of perfect holiness in Buddhism.

3. *Teratai* and *sedap melam* are two flowers that bloom only at midnight.

4. *Gulalei* is a kind of chocolate candy.

5. *Air jahe* is a drink made of coconut sugar and ginger.

Exercise B   *Certain aspects of the Mexican "Day of the Dead" date back to the Aztecs, the Indians who ruled Mexico before the Spaniards arrived. The following sentences deal with some of their beliefs. Use the information in the second sentence to define the italicized word in the first one. Place the adjective clause or appositive right after the word it is defining (right after the italicized word).*

Ex: 1. The *Aztecs* believed that the fate of the soul depended on how a person died. The Aztecs were an ancient Indian civilization.

The Aztecs, <u>an ancient Indian civilization,</u> believed that the fate of the soul depended on how a person died.

2. For example, the warriors who died in battle went to the *third heaven*. It was the Dwelling Place of the Sun.

3. *Tlalocan* was for people who died from water, for example, by drowning. Tlalocan was the second heaven of the Aztecs.

4. Tlalocan was the kingdom of *Tlaloc*. Tlaloc was the rain god.

5. *The fourth heaven* was the children's heaven. The fourth heaven was Chichihuacuauhco.

6. The souls of adults who died from natural causes had to make the difficult journey to *Mictlan*. Mictlan was the kingdom of Mictlantecuhtli.

7. In some villages today it is still possible to see life-sized skeletons of *Mictlantecuhtli*. He was the Lord of the Dead in ancient Mexico.

CYCLE TWO

Practice 3. Example Signals

Defining or explaining an idea is not the only way to make it clear. As you saw in Lesson 2, examples can be used to clarify a general idea by providing specific support:

General: Children wear costumes on Halloween.

Specific: They may dress as cowboys, Superman, or Mickey Mouse.

This specific support is often introduced by an *example signal: for example, for instance, to give an example, to give another example*. These are all *noncombining signals* (Lesson 2, Practice 7):

   a.   Some costumes fulfill wishes. <u>For example</u>, some children will dress as cowboys or Superman because they would like to be like these heroes. Other costumes are humorous. You may, <u>for instance</u>, see Mickey Mouse or even a can of soup walking down the street. <u>To give another example</u>, you might find a world-famous politician, <u>for example</u>, an American president, at your door.

You can see from this example that the example signal may be at the beginning of the sentence or inside the sentence. Notice that the signal is preceded by some kind of punctuation and usually followed by a comma. Students often have difficulty deciding what kind of punctuation to place before example signals (and other kinds of noncombining signals). This error is very common:

b. *Some costumes fulfill wishes, for example, some children will dress as cowboys or Superman.

You can decide what to put before the signal expression by looking carefully at what follows it. If it is followed by a sentence, place a period or a semicolon before it:

sentence →

c. . For example, some children will dress as cowboys or Superman.
(or) ; for example, some children will dress as cowboys or Superman.

If the words that follow the signal are not a complete sentence, place a comma before the signal:

not sentence →

d. You may, for instance, see Mickey Mouse walking down the street.

Another very useful example signal is *such as*, which is different from the others in an important way: It always follows one noun structure and introduces another. In the following examples, the noun structures, which may be either simple or more complex, are underscored.

e. You may see a <u>political figure</u> such as <u>an American president.</u>
adj. + noun

f. You may see a <u>public figure</u> such as <u>the Queen of England.</u>
noun + preposition + noun

g. At a Halloween party you might have a few <u>surprises</u>, such as <u>skeletons that</u>
noun +
<u>jump out from behind doors.</u>
adjective clause

A verb in the *-ing* form (called a *gerund*) may also function as a noun:

h. On Halloween some children play mean <u>tricks</u>, such as <u>throwing eggs.</u>
gerund phrase

There are two common errors to avoid when using *such as*:

i. *Some children play tricks such as <u>they throw eggs.</u>
clause: not a noun structure

j. Some children play tricks. *<u>Such as throwing eggs.</u>
not a complete sentence

Exercise *Write sentences based on the generalizations and specific examples that follow. Try to use a variety of example signals and practice placing them in different sentence positions.*

	Generalization	**Examples**
Ex: 1.	scary costumes	witches, skeletons

Some children wear scary costumes such as black cat or skeleton
costumes.

2.	historical figures	kings, queens
3.	monsters	Frankenstein's monster, Dracula
4.	Disney characters	Mickey Mouse, Donald Duck
5.	treats	candy, cake, fruit
6.	tricks	break pumpkins, put soap on windows, let air out of tires
7.	traditional decorations	pumpkins, corn, witches, ghosts
8.	traditional Halloween foods	pumpkin pie, popcorn, apple cider
9.	traditional party activities	tell ghost stories, bob for apples, have a "haunted house"
10.	haunted house . . . surprises	strange sounds, ghosts that jump out un-expectedly

Practice 4. Directed Writing: Halloween

Write an essay describing Halloween to someone who is not very familiar with
American culture. Be sure to include definitions of terms your reader may not

understand. Use examples to make your ideas clear. One possible way to organize your essay would be as follows:

First Paragraph: Introduction: When? Where? Who? In one or two sentences introduce the major activities: trick-or-treating, parties. Do not define/explain yet.

Second Paragraph: Topic sentence: trick-or-treating. Define/explain it.
Give examples of costumes, tricks, treats.

Third Paragraph: Topic sentence: parties. Food, decorations, activities.
Give examples; define/explain when necessary.

Fourth Paragraph: Short conclusion: Why do you think Halloween is so popular among both children and adults?

ADDING ON

Practice 5. Adjective Clauses: Restrictive and Nonrestrictive

In this course you have practiced two somewhat different kinds of adjective clauses. Adjective clauses like the one in the following example were introduced in Lesson 1 (Practice 7):

a.   The Day of the Dead is especially important for people <u>that have recently lost a loved one.</u>

Adjective clauses like this one are called *restrictive.* In this example you can see that the adjective clause restricts, or specifies, the reference of the word *people:* It identifies which people, of all the people in the world, the sentences are talking about. It is possible to use either *that* or *who/which* in such clauses; notice also that they are not punctuated with commas.
　　The following two adjective clauses, like those in Practice 2 of this lesson, on the other hand, are called *nonrestrictive:*

b.   People may drink tequila or pulque, <u>which are alcoholic drinks made from cactus.</u>

c.   Tlalocan was the kingdom of Tlaloc, <u>who was the rain god.</u>

　　These adjective clauses do not specify which tequila or pulque or which Tlaloc the sentence is talking about. Their function is to define or explain rather than specify. Such adjective clauses do not begin with *that* and must be punctuated with commas, dashes, or parentheses.
　　It is not always easy to decide if an adjective clause is specifying or defining/explaining, but the following techniques are helpful in most cases. First, try asking *some, all,* or *one* questions: Is the Day of the Dead especially important for *some* people, for *all* people or for *one* person? If the answer is *some,* the clause is restrictive. Is *some, all* or *one* tequila made from cactus? Is Tlaloc *some*

gods, *all* gods or *one* god? If the answer is *all* or *one*, the clause is nonrestrictive. Another way to do the same thing is to ask an "identifying" question and see if it makes sense. If it makes sense the clause is restrictive: Which people is the Day of the Dead especially important for? People *that have recently lost a loved one.* If such a question does not make sense, the clause is nonrestrictive: *Which tequila is made from cactus? It all is. *Which Tlaloc was the rain god? There was only one.

Exercise   *In the following essay, the sentences in parentheses can be rewritten as adjective clauses. Some will be restrictive, others nonrestrictive. Rewrite the essay, making the parenthetical sentences adjective clauses. Punctuate the nonrestrictive ones with commas; do not punctuate the restrictive ones. You may use **that** in the restrictive ones but not in the nonrestrictive ones.*

Ex: 1. A holiday (a holiday celebrates the return of the dead) is found in many different cultures.
    A holiday <u>that celebrates the return of the dead</u> is found in many cultures. Such holidays probably date back thousands of years.   2. In ancient Egypt, for example, a Day of the Dead was celebrated at the time of the winter solstice (the winter solstice is when the days are shortest and the nights are longest).   3. This ceremony was in honor of Osiris (Osiris was the Egyptian god of the lower world).   4. Specifically, it was in honor of his death (his death symbolized the death of vegetation). On this day the souls of the dead returned to the land of the living.   5. People prepared food for the dead (the dead would be hungry after their long journey from the underworld). When it began to grow dark, lamps were placed outside the houses.   6. The lamps (the lamps were kept burning all night) made it easy for the wandering souls to find their way home.
    7. It is interesting that many of the things (Americans do things on Halloween) are similar to Egyptian practices thousands of years ago.   8. Halloween (Halloween takes place at the end of the growing season) still has some connection with the "death of vegetation." American children go from house to house asking for treats.   9. This may remind us of the food offerings (the Egyptians set out food offerings for the visiting souls).   10. The carved pumpkins (Americans light them with a candle and put them in front of their houses) may remind us of the lanterns (lanterns lit the way for the returning Egyptian souls).   11. The skeletons, ghosts, and monsters (skeletons, ghosts, and monsters are seen everywhere on Halloween) clearly indicate that the origins of this holiday are very old.

Practice 6. Articles

Nouns can have either general reference or more specific, limited reference. As you have seen (Lesson 2, Practice 12), nouns with general reference often take no article:

   a. Holidays reflect culture. (<u>All holidays, all culture</u>).

The underscored nouns in the following example, however, are limited in reference; they do not refer to all villages, all candy, or all marigolds:

b.   Once I was in <u>a</u> small Mexican <u>village</u> on November 2. I saw <u>candy</u> shaped like skulls and there were <u>marigolds</u> everywhere.

The reference of these nouns is limited but it is not identifiable; that is, we cannot say specifically *which* village, *which* candy, or *which* marigolds are being referred to. The rule for nouns with limited, unidentifiable reference is: use *a* before count/singular nouns (*village*); use no article before count/plural and noncount nouns (*marigolds, candy*)

On the other hand, if a noun's reference is identifiable, use *the*, whether the noun is count or noncount, singular or plural. A noun's reference may be identifiable for a number of different reasons. First, there may be only one possible, or at least likely, reference for a noun. There is only one sun in our solar system and there is only one cemetery in a typical Mexican village:

c.   When <u>the sun</u> went down, people walked to <u>the cemetery</u>.

You can easily answer an identifying question: Which sun? our sun, the only one possible in this context. Second, a noun's reference may be identifiable because preceding or following words make it clear, as in these examples:

d.   <u>The</u> village <u>that we stayed in</u> was far from any big city.

e.   <u>The</u> Indians <u>in that part of Mexico</u> still speak Indian languages.

Again, identifying questions can be answered: Which village? the one *that we stayed in.* Which Indians still speak Indian languages? the ones *in that part of Mexico.* Finally, notice how the articles change in the following example:

f.   I saw <u>candy</u> shaped like skulls and there were <u>marigolds</u> everywhere. <u>The candy</u> and <u>the flowers</u> made the holiday seem lighthearted.

After a noun has been mentioned once its reference is considered identified: The second time *candy* is mentioned it takes the article *the.* Notice also that a different noun with the same reference as one already mentioned takes *the: flowers* clearly refers to *marigolds,* which have already been mentioned. In such cases an identifying question might be answered as follows: Which candy? the candy that has already been mentioned.

The following summary may be helpful.

GENERAL REFERENCE	*LIMITED REFERENCE*			
	Unidentifiable			Identifiable
	Noncount	Count		
		Singular	Plural	
no article	no article	a	no article	the

Article usage is very complicated, and the explanations just given are partial. Nevertheless, they should help you reduce the number of errors you may make.

Exercise   *Fill in the blanks in the following essay with **a, the,** or **0** (nothing). The vocabulary list will help you decide which article to use with unidentified nouns:*

> *Count:*   wedding, family, bride, groom, fortuneteller, house, feast, horse, chestnut, litter, parent
>
> *Noncount:*   value, wine, candy, wealth

THE TRADITIONAL KOREAN WEDDING

The traditional Korean marriage is based on Confucianism, a philosophy which says that people must obey their superiors in all things. Traditionally,

Ex: 1.   therefore, __0__ young people had no say in choosing their marriage partner; their parents decided. Some families still follow these traditional practices.

Ex: 2,3.   First, __the__ bride and groom's parents decide if _____ two families will
   4,5.   get along. If _____ families are satisfied with each other, _____ parents ask
   6,7,8.   _____ fortuneteller if _____ marriage will be successful. If _____ fortuneteller predicts harmony, preparations for _____ wedding can begin.
   9.
   10.   Once the parents decide whether the wedding will take place, _____
   11,12.   bride's parents give _____ feast. _____ bride and groom cannot go because
   13,14.   they cannot show their faces until _____ day of _____ ceremony. When
   15,16,17.   _____ wedding day arrives, _____ bride is carried to the temple on _____
   18.   litter, which is a sort of chair with handles. When they arrive at _____
   19.   ceremony, they have to stand far apart. They say nothing during _____
   20,21.   ceremony. _____ only person who speaks is _____ most respected elder in
   22,23.   _____ family, who reads the traditional text. _____ bride vows four times
   24,25.   to be loyal and obedient; _____ groom vows twice to accept _____ woman
   26,27.   as his wife. When this is done, _____ wine is poured and _____ bride and
   28,29.   groom toast each other. As they do this, _____ parents throw _____
   30,31.   chestnuts or _____ candy to the bride, wishing _____ newlyweds happiness.

Practice 7. Repeating for Clarity: *this* and *these*

You saw in Lesson 2 (Practice 6) that information is sometimes repeated to make the relation between two paragraphs clear. Repetition can also be used to make the relation between sentences in a single paragraph clear. However, too much direct repetition becomes clumsy and distracting:

> a.   *For the Day of the Dead, an altar is set up and decorated, and special foods are prepared. While the altar is set up and decorated, and special foods are prepared, the mood is one of excitement and anticipation.

The idea could be repeated—and the clumsiness avoided—by using *this* or *these* in one of the following ways:

b.   During this period, the mood is one of excitement and anticipation.

c.   While these preparations are going on, the mood is one of excitement and anticipation.

d.   While this is being done, the mood is one of excitement and anticipation.

This and *these* can be used before nouns: *This period, these preparations* (use *this* before a singular noun; *these* before a plural noun). Or, *this* may be used by itself: *While this is being done.* In the last example, notice that *this* is singular but may refer to more than one thing: the altar, the decorations, the special foods.

Used by itself, *this* is especially important in academic writing because it can refer back to a general, or abstract, idea as well as to more specific things:

e.   The Mexican Indian believes that this life is only one stage in the soul's journey. Perhaps this is why death is sometimes treated almost lightly.
(*This* refers to the belief that life is only one stage in the soul's journey.)

Exercise A   *Tell what the words **this** and **these** refer to in the following description of a Muslim holiday.*

EID AL-ADHA

One of the most important holidays in the Muslim world is *Eid Al-*

Ex: 1.   *Adha.* On this day Muslims remember the story of Ibrahim and Ismail. In
2.   this story, Allah orders Ibrahim to sacrifice his son Ismail to prove the
3.   strength of his faith. However, just as Ibrahim is about to do this, Allah tells him to stop. Ibrahim sacrifices a sheep instead to show his gratitude.
4.   To prepare for this holiday, the men go to the sheep market and buy a healthy sheep. Everyone buys new clothes for the holiday. The men also go to the bank to exchange their old money for new money.

On the day of *Eid Al-Adha,* the men go to the mosque to pray and then return home to slaughter the sheep. They give part of the meat to relatives
5.   and to the poor. When this is done, everyone gathers around the oldest member of the family, a grandmother or grandfather, who gives the children some money. Then the family eats and the children usually go out to a
6,7.   movie or to a fair which takes place at this time of the year. All these activities have meaning for Muslims. For example, sacrificing the sheep reminds us that Allah was merciful when Ibrahim obeyed him without
8.   question. This holiday also reminds people of the importance of the family and of being generous to the poor.

Exercise B   *Fill in the blanks in the following essay with **this** or **these**.*

THE FESTIVAL OF THE WEAVERS

The Chinese Festival of the Weavers celebrates the love story of a farmer, Niu-lang, and a fairy weaver, Zhi-nu.

Ex: 1.   According to the story, __these__ lovers were forbidden to marry by the laws of heaven which said that fairies could not marry with people. But one day Zhi-nu snuck out of heaven, flew to earth, and married Niu-lang.

2. _____ made the Creator of the World very angry. He told Zhi-nu that she
3. had broken the laws of heaven and that according to _____ rules she
    would be put to death if she did not return immediately. However, her love
    for Niu-lang was so strong that she refused to return to Heaven. When the
4. Lord of Creation saw _____ his heart was touched and he changed the
    punishment: He separated them by a river and told them they could see
5. each other only once a year. On _____ day, according to legend, all the
    swallows would fly to the river. With their bodies, they would make a bridge
    for Niu-lang and Zhi-nu to cross over on.
6.   To prepare for _____ day we decorate a table with flowers and fruit.
7. Girls also put cosmetics on the table for Zhi-nu to use. They do _____
    because they think that if Zhi-nu uses their cosmetics, they will become more
    beautiful. On the evening of the holiday, girls put on their most beautiful
    dresses and pray for a good harvest, beauty, and the ability to weave good
    cloth.
8.   As you can see from _____ description, the Festival of the Weavers is
9. rather old-fashioned and I am not sure if young women still do _____
    things.

Practice 8. Restatement Signals; *that is* and *in other words*

In this lesson you have practiced using adjective clauses and appositives to include definition of terms or ideas that might not be clear to your reader. The
noncombining signal expressions *that is* and *in other words* have a similar function.
They introduce a restatement or a kind of clarifying repetition. If you feel an
idea will not be clear, you may want to restate or repeat it in different words:

a. On Halloween everyone makes a jack o'lantern, <u>that is,</u> a hollow pumpkin with a
    face carved in it.

b. As a Halloween trick someone might soap your windows; <u>in other words,</u> someone
    might take a bar of soap and smear your windows.

Remember, if a noncombining expression introduces a word or a phrase, it is
punctuated with commas (example a). If it introduces a clause, it is preceded by a
period or a semicolon (example b).
    Note: Do not confuse structures introduced by the restatement signal
that is with adjective clauses:

c. A trick <u>that is very popular</u> is soaping windows.
                adjective clause

Exercise Add definition or explanation to the following sentences. Decide what punctuation to
place before the restatement signal—it will depend on what you write **after** the signal.

Ex: 1. Setting out food for the spirits is a continuation of an ancient Indian prac-
            tice; in other words, <u>Mexican Indians have been doing this for centuries.</u>

Ex: 2.   A popular activity at Halloween parties is bobbing for apples, that is, <u>trying to remove an apple from a basin of water using only your teeth.</u>

3.   On Halloween children expect to get treats __ in other words _____
_____.

4.   If they do not get a treat, they might play a trick__ that is _____
_____.

5.   At Halloween parties there is often a costume contest __ in other words
_____.

6.   At some parties a part of the house is supposed to be haunted __ that is
_____.

7.   On the Day of the Dead many Mexicans "feed" the returning spirits __ that is _____.

8.   In the graveyard they might act out scenes from the dead person's life __ in other words _____.

9.   The mood in the cemetery becomes more relaxed as bottles of tequila are passed around __ in other words _____.

Practice 9. The Present Tenses

The present tenses are used to describe repeated or habitual actions such as those in this lesson: Children do more or less the same thing every Halloween. There are four present tenses: the simple present, the present progressive, the present perfect, and the present perfect progressive.

The *simple present tense* indicates that two or more things happen at the same time or that one follows the other. It is, therefore, the basic tense for describing a sequence of actions:

   a.   Children <u>put</u> on their costumes and then <u>go</u> from house to house. At each house they <u>say</u> "trick or treat" when someone <u>opens</u> the door.

Check your writing to make sure you have put an *-s* on verbs in the third person singular: someone open*s* . . .

The *present progressive* indicates that one action begins before a second one and is not yet completed when the second one occurs:

   b.   When the bride and groom arrive at the church, everyone <u>is waiting</u>.

In other words, they got to the church before the bride and groom and they are still there (waiting) when the bride and groom arrive. Make sure you have used the correct form of *be* (*am, is,* or *are*) and have added *-ing* to the main verb.

Both the *present perfect* and the *present perfect progressive* may be used to show *how long* an action has been in progress:

c.   Mexican Indians <u>have observed</u> a Day of the Dead <u>for centuries.</u>

d.   <u>In recent years</u> more and more adults <u>have been dressing</u> up and <u>going</u> to Halloween parties.

Check to be sure you have used *has* or *have* correctly (*has* for the third person singular). In the present perfect, be sure you have used the correct past participle—they are often irregular. In the present perfect progressive, do not forget *been* or *-ing*.

The *present perfect* can also be used to emphasize that one action is finished before another begins (if this is not already clear from the context):

e.   When everyone <u>has eaten,</u> the father of the bride makes a speech.

Exercise   *Proofread the following essay and correct any verb tense errors you find.*

THE TRADITIONAL PALESTINIAN MARRIAGE

The traditional Palestinian marriage may differ a bit from village to

Ex: village. Basically, however, it <u>is change</u> very little for as long as anyone

has changed

remember. In most villages the traditional ceremony begin on "al-Shra," which is the night before the marriage.

On this night there is a party, usually at the groom's house. There a band, and everyone sing folksongs and dance the "al-Dabka," which is a traditional Palestinian folk dance. For this party the groom's family provide candy and tea or coffee.

The next day, which is called "al-Zafa," the people walk from the groom's house to the bride's house singing and dancing. When they reaching the bride's house, the bride and her family waiting. The "Chitl," that is, the Muslim holy man, is also wait. He ask both the bride and the groom if they agree to marry each other. Then he read a passage from the Koran, the Muslim Holy Book. When he finishes, the bride and the groom getting into a specially decorated car while the people still singing. Then they return to the groom's house again.

There the groom's parents give everyone a meal. After the meal everyone give the groom some money. When they do this, they go home so the bride and groom can leave on their honeymoon.

Practice 10. The Simple Present Passive

The passive is used when the writer wishes to emphasize *what* is done rather than *who* does it. This focus—what rather than who—is especially common in formal academic writing.

To describe a traditional event (repeated actions), you would most often use the *simple present passive:* be + past participle.

    a.   A special dish <u>is prepared</u>.

    b.   Traditional prayers <u>are said</u>.

Most often the passive is used when it is not necessary to mention who does the action. If it is necessary to mention the doer, use a *by* phrase:

    c.   Religious songs <u>are sung</u> <u>by the priests</u>.

Notice how a passive sentence is related to an active one:

    d.   active: People prepare <u>special foods</u> for the holiday.
                                object
         passive: <u>Special foods</u> are prepared for the holiday.
                  subject

As you can see, the object of an active sentence becomes the subject of the passive one. If you decide to change an active sentence to the passive, be sure you can identify the whole object phrase:

    e.   People prepare <u>the *pan de muerto,* which is a special bread with the dead person's name on it.</u>
        <u>The *pan de muerto,* which is a special bread with the dead person's name on it</u>, is prepared.

The whole object, even if it is long, is moved to the subject position. Do not leave part of it behind:

    f.   *The <u>pan de muerto</u> is prepared, which is a special bread with the dead person's name on it.

Exercise A   *Fill in the blanks in the following paragraphs with the simple present passive of the verbs in parentheses.*

THE LUNAR NEW YEAR CELEBRATION IN VIET NAM

The Vietnamese and Chinese celebrate Tet (the lunar new year) at the end of January or the beginning of February. People celebrate by going to the pagoda, wearing new clothes, decorating their houses, and eating traditional meals.

Ex: 1.   A week before this holiday the houses (decorate) <u>are decorated</u> in red,

2.   and branches of cherry blossoms (add) _____ for good luck. Traditional dishes like *banh chung* (rice cake filled with meat and soybean curd)

3.   (prepare) _____ during this week. Another traditional food is cold

4.   seasoned pork, which (serve) _____ with pickled onions or cabbage. At the same time, new clothes (buy) _____ or (make) _____

5,6.

7.   _____. During these days the streets (crowd) _____ with peo-

8.   ple, and the sound of firecrackers (hear) _____ continuously.

Exercise B   *Rewrite the second and third paragraphs of the following essay, making the verbs passive. All the clauses can be made passive **except** the ones that are in italics: Do not change them. Decide if it is necessary to add a **by** phrase, to tell who is doing these things. Be careful to move the whole object to the subject position in the passive sentence.*

JAPAN'S OBON FESTIVAL

The Japanese celebrate a festival called *Obon* every summer. It is a festival for the spirits of the dead, who return home on this day. Everyone welcomes them and celebrates their return.

Ex: 1.   We must do many things to prepare for their return.   2. Women clean the houses very carefully.

   <u>Many things are done to prepare for their return. The houses are cleaned very carefully.</u>

3. They clean the small family shrines especially carefully.   4. Sometimes they make figures of animals such as horses or cows out of cucumbers and bamboo sticks.   5. They place these animals on the family shrine, *so that the returning spirits will have a way to return to the land of the dead when their visit is finished.*   6. The women also prepare traditional foods such as Chirashi-sushi, a special rice dish.

7. While the women do these things, the men sometimes decorate the main entrance door.   8. They decorate it with colorful flowers and plants *so the spirits will want to enter.*

ADDITIONAL WRITING TOPICS

1. Describe a traditional holiday in your country. Be sure to define or explain any terms or ideas which might not be clear and provide examples if they will help the reader understand.

2. Describe a ceremony in your culture, for example, a baptism, a wedding, or a funeral.

3. Describe the typical or traditional pattern of courtship in your country.

4. Describe a religious service in the religion you know best. For example, what do people do when they go to a church, synagogue, mosque, shrine, or temple?

5. Describe a day in the life of a typical villager in your country (if there is such a thing as a typical villager in your country).

Lesson 4

DESCRIBING AND EXPLAINING

Subject: Architecture and Design

Contents:

INTRODUCTION

Lessons 2 and 3 introduced the basic concepts of support and clarity. In this lesson you will see how these ideas apply to two more specific writing tasks: describing and explaining.

Cycle One begins with a reading about an unusual architectural design, which is briefly described. The idea is then explained; reasons are given to support, or justify, the unfamiliar design. You will see what techniques are used to make the description clear and will write a paragraph of description yourself.

In Cycle Two you will design a structure and then describe and explain it. You will support your idea not with examples but with explanation—with your reasons for designing the structure as you have.

Adding On introduces a number of exercises on paragraph organization, sentence building and variety, and punctuation.

CYCLE ONE

Practice 1. Reading

A COMMUNITY FOR THE FUTURE

1   Buckminster Fuller, an American inventor and designer, once proposed an unusual community to house thousands of people and replace the depressed neighborhoods of East St. Louis. He called his design the Old Man River City Project.

5   Fuller's proposed community (see Figure 4-1) is a moonlike crater, a mile in diameter at the base. Both the inner and outer sides of the crater would be covered with terraces. On the outer terraces, there would be individual apartments with private balconies and small gardens. The inner terraces would be used for communal activities such as

10   shopping, education, recreation, and entertainment. Roads, parking, public transportation, and other such necessities would be out of sight—either underground or inside the walls of the crater. Over the whole crater, there would be a raised geodesic covering, a kind of huge umbrella protecting the city.

15   Fuller had clear practical reasons for designing an entirely original community. First, people would live as close together as in any large city, but they would have more privacy because their apartments would be located on the outer circumference of a huge circle, facing outwards, each with a clear view. At the same time, it would be very easy to walk

20   "downtown," that is, to the inner terraces, where all public activities would be conveniently close together. Another advantage of the community would be the nearly pollution-free environment. Because automobiles, trucks, and other means of transportation would be hidden, there would be little visual, air, or sound pollution. Moreover, the cli-

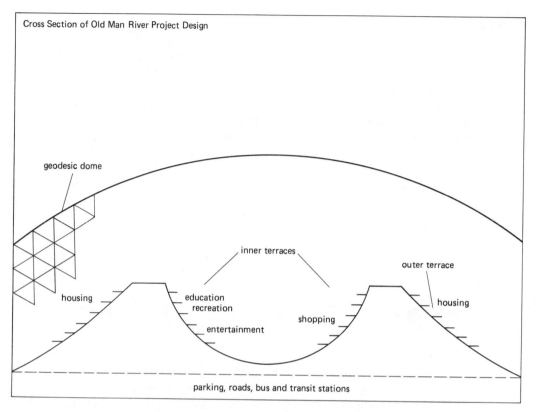

Cross Section of Old Man River Project Design

geodesic dome

inner terraces

outer terrace

housing

education
recreation

entertainment

shopping

housing

parking, roads, bus and transit stations

Figure 4–1

25   mate would be improved: The geodesic dome would let in the sunlight
but keep out the rain, wind, and snow. Finally, Fuller's project would be
cheaper to build than the same number of apartments in traditional
apartment buildings. For all these reasons, Fuller was convinced that
someday such a community would be built.

Questions
1. Where would the apartments be? Why?
2. Where would the buses be? Why?
3. Where would the theaters and stores be? Why?
4. Why would there be an "umbrella" over the community?
5. How many reasons for building a community like this are given in the last
   paragraph?
6. Can you think of any other advantages? Any disadvantages?
7. Would you like to live in this kind of community?

Practice 2. Clarity: Repetition and Position Signals

Description seems easier to write than it is: You must do all you can to make a
description precise and clear. As you have seen in earlier lessons, one way to

make writing clear is to repeat certain information; another is to use signal expressions, expressions which make the logic and organization obvious. Notice, first, how information is repeated in the first two sentences of the second paragraph in the introductory reading:

a. <u>Fuller's proposed community</u> is a moonlike <u>crater</u>, a mile in diameter at the base.
              repeated   new
    Both the inner and outer sides of the <u>crater</u> would be covered with <u>terraces</u>.
                               repeated   new

In this example, the first sentence contains a paragraph bridge (*Fuller's proposed community* refers back to the introduction, where the idea is first presented) and new information: The community would be shaped like a crater. The second sentence repeats the word *crater* before introducing the new information: It would be covered with terraces. This step-by-step organization allows the reader to follow a complicated piece of writing. It relates the new information to what the reader already knows—the repeated information—and in general the structure looks like this:

    First Sentence: Repeated   New
    Second Sentence: Repeated   New
    Third Sentence: Repeated   New

The repeated precedes the new: It is usually in the first half of the sentence.
    The second way to make meaning clear is to provide signal expressions. In description it is especially important to make clear where things are in relation to one another. Any words or expressions that do this can be called *position signals*. Often, but not always, they are prepositional phrases: next to the door, under the window, and so on. Position signals, like repeated information, are often placed in the first half of the sentence:

b. Fuller's proposed community is a moonlike crater, a mile in diameter at the base. Both the <u>inner</u> and the <u>outer</u> sides of the crater would be covered with terraces. <u>On the outer</u> terraces, there would be individual apartments. . . .

Exercise   *Go through the rest of the second paragraph of the reading. Circle each word or phrase that repeats information and underline the position signals. Which sentence does not follow the pattern:* known (+ position signal) . . . new?

Practice 3. There Is/There Are

Before beginning more complicated writing tasks, it might be a good idea to practice using *there is* and *there are*—two of the most common structures in description. Notice that the choice of *is* or *are* depends on whether the following noun is singular or plural:

a. There <u>is</u> a large <u>deck</u> behind the house.

b. There <u>are</u> several large <u>windows</u> in front.

Students often write sentences like the two following ones, but they should be avoided. The first is incorrect and the second is usually too informal for academic writing:

    c. *It has a large deck in front of the house.

    d. *You can see a large deck in front of the house.

Notice also that it is possible to leave out the word *there* if the sentence begins with a prepositional phrase indicating position:

    e. Behind the house <u>there</u> is a large deck.

    f. Behind the house   is a large deck.

Exercise *Use the following information to write a paragraph. Place the position signals (the prepositional phrases) in the first part of each sentence.*

Ex: 1. large fireplace   in the middle of the room
           <u>In the middle of the room there is a large fireplace</u>.

Ex: 2. large painting   above the fireplace
           <u>Above the fireplace is a large painting</u>.

      3. a brass candlestick   on each side of the painting

      4. a coffee table   in front of the fireplace

      5. armchairs   around the coffee table

      6. reading lamps   next to the armchairs

      7. usually a roaring fire   in the fireplace

Practice 4. Ordering Information

Even if you carefully use position signals and repeat information, a description will not be clear if the parts of the thing described are not presented in some logical order, some order that will make sense to the reader. It would not, for example, make any sense to begin a description of the Taj Mahal (in Agra, India) in this way:

    a. *In the front right corner of the Taj Mahal there is a narrow tower. In front of the whole building there is a long pool of water.

Figure 4–2

It does not make sense to begin with a tower; it does not make sense to jump from a tower to the pool of water in front.

In this exercise you will write a paragraph describing the Taj Mahal. Before you begin writing, decide in what order you will mention the following (do not mention them in the order given here):

four towers, large dome, low wall, two small domes,
large arch, pool of water, eight small arches.

Do you want to begin with the most noticeable thing and continue to the least noticeable? Do you want to begin in the middle and work outwards? At the top and work down? At the bottom and work up? Do you want to mix these possible orders? Decide before you begin.

Use position signals, repeat information, and use *there is/there are*. Write a general introductory sentence: a topic sentence telling what you are going to describe.

CYCLE TWO

Practice 5. Designing a House

Draw a picture of either the interior *or* the exterior (not both) of the house you would design for yourself if you had all the money you needed. Draw it carefully but do not put in too much detail. Consider such things as size, shape, building material, number and position of rooms, style (modern, traditional, and so on). Would your house have any unusual features? Use your imagination: You can have anything you want.

If you want to understand the importance of clarity in description, try this when you have finished drawing: Describe your house to someone who will try to draw it as you speak. (Of course you must describe it to someone who has not seen your drawing.)

Practice 6. Directed Writing

Write an essay describing and explaining or justifying the house you have just designed. Turn in your drawing with the essay. Here is a possible way to organize your essay:

First Paragraph: Short introduction: style, size, shape, material, location.

Second Paragraph: Description: parts of the house and their position in relation to one another. Consider how to organize before you begin.

Third Paragraph: Explanation: Why would you like this house? What would its advantages be?

Note: Because this house does not exist (yet) you will need to use modal auxiliaries like *will, would, may, might.* If you are confident that someday this house will exist, use *will, may,* or *might.* If, however, you think that you are just dreaming, that your design is unrealistic, use *would* and *might* (not *will* or *may*). This distinction is explained more fully later in the lesson, but here are two examples for now:

    a.   There <u>will</u> be a large swimming pool in the back yard and I <u>may</u> (or <u>might</u>) build tennis courts too. (<u>Confident</u>.)

    b.   There <u>would</u> be a large swimming pool in the back yard and I <u>might</u> build tennis courts too. (<u>Dreaming</u>.)

ADDING ON

Practice 7. The List Paragraph

The last paragraph of the introductory reading begins, "Fuller had clear practical reasons for designing an entirely original community." The rest of the paragraph supports—or explains—this idea by giving those reasons: privacy, views, convenient public areas, reduced pollution, climate control, low cost.

A paragraph that gives several equally important pieces of information—several reasons, several examples, several problems—can be called a *list paragraph:* It presents the reader with a list.

It is an extremely common type of paragraph, one that is used in quite different kinds of writing. A group of *noncombining* expressions, which may be called *list signals,* can be used to make this organization clear to the reader. They indicate that you are adding new information, or continuing your "list." Some of the most common noncombining list signals are

first, second . . . ; finally; also; in addition; furthermore; moreover

    a.   The geodesic dome would control the climate and reduce heating costs. It would, <u>moreover,</u> be relatively inexpensive to build.

Such expressions, remember, do not combine clauses grammatically. Avoid the following comma error (run-on sentence):

    b.   *The geodesic dome would control the climate and reduce heating costs, <u>also</u> it would be inexpensive to build.

As you may have noticed already in this lesson, the expressions *one . . ./another . . .* are also list signals:

    c.   <u>One interesting feature</u> of the Old Man River Project is the privacy of the apartments, each with a view. <u>Another advantage</u> is that the public places would be conveniently located.

Exercise   *Figure 4-3 is one student's drawing of his ideal country home. Following the drawing is a list of the reasons he gave for liking this house. Use these notes to write a list paragraph. You may not want to use the information in the order in which it is given. Use some list signals, but you do not need to use one in every sentence. Begin the paragraph with a general, or topic, sentence which will make the purpose of the paragraph clear.*

The House's Good Features
1. natural area, scenery
2. built from natural material: wood
3. A-shape matches mountains
4. decks and skylight for sun
5. decks for resting, eating outdoors
6. solar heating
7. dock for fishing, swimming, boating

Student's "Dream House"

Figure 4–3

Practice 8. Gerunds and Complex Noun Phrases

The subjects and objects of verbs are often fairly simple noun phrases, as in this sentence:

> a.   A <u>huge geodesic umbrella</u> would cover the <u>crater</u>.
>   subject   object

The subject in this sentence is an adjective-noun combination, and the object is a simple noun. Other more complicated structures, such as *clauses, gerund phrases,* and *complex noun phrases,* may also function as subjects and objects. An awareness of these structures will increase the choices open to you as a writer.

Clauses

A full clause, often introduced by the word *that,* may function as the subject or object of many verbs, including the verb *be:*

> b.   One of the things that surprised people was <u>that Fuller proposed to cover the whole community with an "umbrella."</u>

Gerund Phrases

A phrase containing a gerund (the *-ing* form of a verb) may also function as a subject or object. Notice that if the gerund phrase itself has a subject, it is in the possessive (Fuller*'s*):

    c. <u>Fuller's proposing to cover the whole community with an "umbrella"</u> is an interesting idea.

Complex Noun Phrases

One common type of complex noun phrase has the form *noun + of + noun:*

    d. One of the best things about Fuller's design would be <u>the elimination of traffic from public places.</u>

Exercise A   *Change the italicized clauses in the following sentences to gerund phrases. Notice that gerunds do not show tense; therefore it is sometimes necessary to change the main verb to capture the meaning of the original clause, as in the example:*

Ex: 1. For many people the most interesting thing about Fuller's dome <u>is</u> *that it would keep out the rain and snow.*
For many people the most interesting thing about Fuller's dome <u>would be</u> its keeping out the rain and snow.

    2. A good reason for building a dome is *that it would reduce the use of energy.*

    3. *That Fuller proposed to put transportation underground* appealed to many people.

    4. One of the things that was important to Fuller was *that everyone have some privacy.*

    5. *That he believed difficult problems can be solved with imagination* is what makes Buckminster Fuller so interesting.

    6. Some people say that the worst thing would be *that they would feel trapped inside a huge bubble.*

Exercise B   *Change the italicized clauses in the following sentences to complex noun phrases. Again, it might be necessary to change the form of the main verb, as in the example:*

Ex: 1. One of the advantages of Fuller's community <u>is</u> *that its public places would be convenient.*
One of the advantages of Fuller's community <u>would be</u> *the convenience of its public places.*

2.   One thing people might not like is *that the surroundings would be unfamiliar.*

3.   Another thing that would bother some people is *that the population would be dense.*

4.   *That the climate would be unnatural* would also bother some.

5.   What appeals to some people is *that the design is simple.*

6.   The only thing people agree on is *that Fuller was an original thinker.*

Practice 9. Repeating for Clarity: *Such*

In Lesson 3 (Practice 7) you saw that the words *this* and *these* can be used to repeat an idea:

   a.   My dream house would be on a lake in the mountains and have skylights, large windows, and a deck extending out over the water. In <u>this</u> house the problems of daily life would seem far away.

It is much more efficient to say *this house* than to repeat all the information about the location, the skylight, the windows, and the deck.
   If the writer were less certain about the dream house, he or she might write:

   b.   My dream house might be on a lake in the mountains and have skylights, large windows, and a deck extending out over the water. In a house <u>such as this</u> the problems of daily life would seem far away.

In this last sentence the writer is indicating that this house is an example of the kind of house he or she would like. The dream house would be something similar to this but perhaps not exactly the same.
Another pattern with *such* has the same meaning:

   c.   It might have skylights, large windows, and a deck extending out over the water. In <u>such a house</u> the problems of daily life would seem far away.

When using either of these patterns with *such,* pay attention to whether the noun modified is count or noncount, singular or plural. Here is a summary of the two patterns:

such a house	(or)	a house such as <u>this</u>	(*Count, singular.*)
such houses		houses such as <u>these</u>	(*Count, plural.*)
such scenery		scenery such as <u>this</u>	(*Noncount.*)

Exercise In the following sentences change the italicized information to **such** phrases.

Ex: 1. Solar heating is becoming cheaper and more efficient. *Developments of this kind* are making more homeowners consider solar heating.
... *Such* developments (or developments *such as these*) are making more homeowners consider solar heating.

2. Solar heating, however, requires sunlight and heats water more slowly than gas and electricity. Because of *problems like these,* people hesitate to install solar heating.

3. Because natural resources are limited, it might be a good idea for the government to spend more on research into natural sources of energy: the sun, the wind, the tides. *This kind of research* would save money in the future.

4. Space stations and even underwater communities have been designed. In planning *communities like these,* designers must take into consideration psychological factors.

5. Human communities in outer space are familiar to readers of science fiction; *settlements of this type,* however, may actually exist some day.

6. It is clear that Fuller's Old Man River Project would be superior to the conventional city in many ways; nevertheless, many people object that *a city like this* would be unpleasant to live in.

7. The Old Man River Project is so unusual that it is doubtful the money will ever be found to build *a community like it.*

8. Slowly, however, people may become accustomed to *this kind of thinking.*

Practice 10. Adjective Clauses: *That, Which, Where*

You have practiced writing adjective clauses beginning with the combining pronouns *who, which,* and *that.* Another combining pronoun, *where,* is especially
useful in writing physical description, but presents some special problems.
Notice that it is correct in the first of the following sentences, but not in the
second:

    a.   The building <u>where he works</u> is famous for its design.

    b.   *The house <u>where he bought</u> is large.

In both of these sentences the adjective clause refers to a place (*the building, the
house*). However, *where* may only be used if it replaces, and functions as, an
adverbial.

    c.   The building is famous. He works <u>in the building</u>.
                                         adverbial
       The building <u>where</u> he works is famous.
                 adverbial

That or *which,* however, must be used if the replaced word is a subject or object:

    d.   The house is large. He bought <u>the house</u>.
                                   object
       The house (<u>that</u>) he bought is large.
         object

It is usually easy to recognize an adverbial of place. With a few exceptions like
the words *here* and *there,* adverbials of place are prepositional phrases: *in the
building, in New York.*

    It is possible, but not necessary, to use *where* in adverbials of place; *that*
and *which* may also be used. There are, however, small but important
differences:

    e.   The building <u>where</u> he works is famous.
       The building <u>that</u> he works <u>in</u> is famous.
       The building <u>which</u> he works <u>in</u> is famous.
       The building <u>in which</u> he works is famous.

No preposition is used with *where;* a preposition must be used with *that* or *which.*
It is formal style to place the preposition before the combining pronoun (*in
which*).

    Where is most often used to replace adverbials with the prepositions *in, on,* and *at.* Other prepositions often express a precise meaning which would be lost if *where* were used:

  f.   There would be a large fireplace <u>over which</u> I would hang my favorite painting.

  g.   Leading to the house would be a long path <u>on each side of which</u> I would plant roses.

Notice that in examples such as these it is clearer to use the formal style, to place the preposition or prepositional phrase before the combining pronoun.

Exercise A   *Combine the following pairs of clauses into one sentence using **that, which,** or **where.** Make the second clause in each pair the adjective clause. (There is often more than one way to do it.)*

Ex. 1.   There is a deck . . . we could eat on the deck.
    There is a deck <u>where we could eat.</u>
    (or) There is a deck <u>that we could eat on.</u>

  2.   There would be a large glass door . . . it would open to let in the air.

  3.   I would have a large garden . . . I would grow vegetables in the garden.

  4.   In the living room there would be a huge skylight . . . it would let the sunlight in.

  5.   There would be a large fireplace . . . above the fireplace there would be a large painting.

  6.   In front of the fireplace there would be a coffee table . . . there would be armchairs around the coffee table.

7. The traditional Latin American home is built around a patio . . . the family can relax in private in the patio.

8. The home is built around a patio . . . the patio cannot be seen from the street.

Exercise B *Fill in the blanks in the following paragraph with **that, which,** or **where** or leave them empty. In some cases there will be more than one possibility.*

MY DREAM HOUSE

     For me the most important part of my dream house would be the large patio and garden. In my living room there would be large glass doors

Ex: 1,2. <u>which (or that)</u> would open directly onto a large patio _____ I would spend as much time as possible. In the patio, I would have a large
3.   redwood table _____ we could use for eating outdoors. I would
4.   also have some comfortable chairs and chaises longues _____ I could spend sunny days reading and sleeping. When it got really hot, I
5.   would jump into the swimming pool _____ would be just off the patio and surrounded with large shade trees. I would also plant a large
6.   garden _____ I would grow vegetables and flowers. At the far end
7.   of the garden, I would plant fruit trees, from _____ I would get my own apples, pears, and plums.

Exercise C *In the following student essay there are several very short sentences and many run-ons (sentences improperly connected with commas). Use adjective clauses to combine some of the short sentences and to fix the run-on sentences. Note: Many of these adjective clauses will be nonrestrictive; they should be punctuated with commas.*

THE TRADITIONAL CHINESE HOUSE

Ex: The traditional Chinese house has a steep roof, it is covered with tiles.

The traditional Chinese house has a steep roof, <u>which is covered with tiles.</u>

     There are four thick columns, one at each corner of the house. The columns support the roof. The walls are made of mud or clay, they are painted white. Usually there are four windows made of wood frames and paper. The door is also made of wood. The door is very heavy.
     Inside, the construction is based on wood. The floors are made of wood, they are painted red. There are four rooms in the house. As you enter the first is the dining room, there is a bedroom on each side of the dining room. Of course there is also a kitchen. In the kitchen there are often small altars, images of To-Di-Shan (the kitchen god) are placed on these altars.

Practice 11. Modals and Verbs: The Future

In writing about the house you designed, you saw that the choice of *will* or *would* depends on whether you view a future situation as a realistic one—one which may in fact occur—or an unrealistic one—one which will not occur, which is imaginary or hypothetical.

Modals are often used to express the degree of certainty a speaker or writer feels about something. Something may be considered quite certain or only possible. The modals *will, may, might,* and *could* can be used to express these degrees of certainty in realistic situations:

> Certain: will
> ↑   may
> ↓   might
> Possible: could

Will expresses certainty; *may* expresses somewhat stronger possibility than *might,* and *might* is a bit stronger than *could.* An architect discussing a house that is being built (realistic situation) might say,

> a.   There <u>will</u> be a lot of room to add on. The owners <u>may</u> want to add a deck. They <u>might</u> want a swimming pool. They <u>could</u> even build a guest cottage in back.

It is also possible to express degree of certainty in a hypothetical situation, but the choice of modal is somewhat different. *Will* changes to *would* and *may* to *might* so that there are only three possibilities:

> Certain: would
> ↑   might
> Possible: could

A person dreaming about an ideal house might say,

> b.   There <u>would</u> be a lot of room to add on. I <u>might</u> want to add a deck. I <u>might</u> want a swimming pool. I <u>could</u> even build a guest cottage in back.

Modals may express meanings besides certainty or possibility. *Can,* for example, expresses ability or opportunity in a realistic situation. The architect might say,

> c.   The owners may want a swimming pool so they <u>can</u> swim after work.

The dreamer, however, would have to use *could:*

> d.   I would build a pool so I <u>could</u> swim.

These meanings are summarized in the table on p. 76.

Notice that the first verb form following a modal is always in the simple form: There will *be;* it would *have;* he may *add;* they could *be* working; he might *have* gone. Avoid this type of error:

> *it will *has;* he may *working.*

MEANING	REALISTIC SITUATION	HYPOTHETICAL SITUATION
Certainty	will ⟶	would
↕	may ⟶	might
	might	
Possibility	could	could
Ability/Opportunity	can ⟶	could

The reality or unreality of a situation affects not only the choice of modal but also the tense of verbs occurring after combining signals like *if* and *when*. The following sentences refer to a hypothetical future situation, but the underscored verbs are in the past tense. In these sentences the past tense indicates unreality rather than past time:

> e. I could build more rooms <u>if</u> I <u>wanted</u> them. I could relax on the deck <u>when</u> I <u>got</u> home.

Exercise *The following paragraph is written as if it describes a realistic situation. Rewrite it so that it describes a hypothetical situation. Pay attention to both modals and verb tense.*

Ex: 1,2. The house ~~will~~ *would* be Spanish style, built around a patio. The walls <u>will</u> be

3,4. thick and made of earth so that if it <u>is</u> hot outside, it <u>will</u> stay cool inside.

5,6. There <u>will</u> be a very modern kitchen so that I <u>can</u> enjoy my hobby, cooking.

7,8. There <u>will</u> be four or five small bedrooms so people <u>can</u> come for the

9,10,11. weekend. When guests <u>come</u>, they <u>will</u> do nothing but relax. That <u>will</u> be

12,13,14. my house rule. I <u>will</u> do all the cooking while they <u>rest</u> in the patio or <u>swim</u>.

15,16. When the weather <u>is</u> bad, they <u>can</u> read in front of the fireplace or, if they

17. <u>prefer</u>, listen to music, watch movies, or play cards.

Practice 12. Commas and Semicolons

The comma has a variety of uses, some of which you have already seen in previous lessons. To begin with, nonrestrictive adjective clauses and appositives are set off from the rest of the sentence by commas:

> a. The Taj Mahal, (which is) one of the most beautiful buildings in the world, is in Agra, India.

Introductory phrases and clauses, especially if they are long, are separated from the rest of the sentence by a comma:

> b. As you passed from the hallway into the living room, you would see the fireplace.

    c. On each side of the path leading to the front door, I would plant a row of rosebushes.

Clauses connected with *and, but, so, or, nor, for,* and *yet* are generally separated by a comma, especially if the first clause is long:

    d. Guests could go swimming in the pool that would be just off the patio, or they might prefer to just relax in the garden.

Items in a series are also separated by commas:

    e. In the garden there would be chairs, chaises longues, a picnic table, and a barbecue pit.

You have also seen that noncombining signal expressions (like *for example, in other words, furthermore, in addition*) are separated from the rest of the sentence with commas (example f) unless they introduce a new sentence (example g):

    f. Fuller's geodesic umbrella would make the climate more agreeable and, furthermore, reduce energy costs.

    g. Fuller's geodesic umbrella would make the climate more agreeable. Furthermore, it would reduce energy costs.

The semicolon does not indicate as strong a break in ideas as a period does. For this reason it is often used with noncombining signals, which indicate a close logical relationship, such as addition (example h) or exemplification (example i):

    h. Fuller's geodesic umbrella would make the climate more agreeable; furthermore, it would reduce energy costs.

    i. In Fuller's project, public places would be located in the central area; stores, theaters, and schools, for example, would all be on the inner terraces.

Semicolons may, of course, be used in sentences without noncombining signal expressions provided that there is a close logical connection between the two clauses:

    j. Fuller's geodesic umbrella would make the climate more agreeable; it would reduce energy costs.

Exercise   *Fill in the blanks in the following sentences with commas, semicolons, or periods. If no punctuation is required leave the blank empty or write in the symbol for nothing: Ø. There may be more than one possibility in some cases. Note: If you find you have sentences longer than about thirty words, you may be overusing the semicolon.*

or: For example,

Ex: 1. Architecture may reflect culture; for example, the traditional Spanish house, which is built around a patio, may express a certain attitude toward the family and toward the public. It gives its back to the street, that is, the public, but it opens onto the patio, which is the center of family life.

    2. In the garden __ I would plant flowers __ herbs __ and fruit trees.

    3. The Spanish house looks inward __ the American house looks outward.

4. To take advantage of the natural setting __ my dream house would have large windows __ skylights __ and outdoor living spaces __ in other words __ a deck __ and a patio.

5. I would relax in the patio __ after a long day at work.

6. He likes large houses __ but she prefers small ones.

7. Unlike the Spanish-style house __ the American house usually faces the street __ if there is a fence __ it is usually not high enough to hide the house from the public __ this might be related in some way to the American ideal of "neighborliness" __ that is __ to the idea that people who live close to one another should be open __ friendly __ and helpful.

8. We have traditionally thought of houses as solid __ fixed __ immovable __ structures __ but other cultures have sometimes thought of the house differently __ the traditional Japanese house __ for example __ has sliding walls and windows that can be removed from the wall to let in the air __ nomadic cultures __ to give another example __ have always thought of the house __ that is __ the tent __ as something to pack up and move around.

Practice 13. Singular and Plural

A number of the "small" errors the average student makes are related to singular/plural usage. These errors may concern nouns:

a. *The house has two large window.

Or they may concern the relation between subject and verb, a third person singular subject often taking a special verb form:

b. *The house have two large windows.

Many noun errors can be spotted in careful proofreading but others are caused by confusion concerning *count* and *noncount nouns* (Lesson 1, Practice 9). Noncount nouns have no plural form:

c. *Bricks are made from mud<u>s.</u>

Bricks are countable: They have shape, they are separable. Mud is not countable: It is shapeless, unseparable—until it is made into bricks.

Errors in subject-verb agreement are often easier to avoid—or to find. In several tenses, remember, there is a special form for the third person singular:

d. He eat<u>s</u> too much. He ha<u>s</u> already eaten three hamburgers and now he i<u>s</u> eating another. He wa<u>s</u> sick yesterday but he keep<u>s</u> on eating too much.

Certain types of sentences, however, present more problems than those just given. First, if a noun is followed by another noun in a prepositional phrase, the verb will agree with the first noun:

e. The <u>construction</u> of skyscrapers <u>is</u> extremely complicated.

f. The <u>designs</u> for the house <u>are</u> fascinating.

On the other hand, if a quantity expression is followed by a noun in a prepositional phrase, the verb will agree with the noun unless the quantity expression is
one:

   g.   One of the houses <u>was</u> built by a famous architect.

   h.   Some of the <u>houses are</u> for sale.

   i.   A lot of the <u>land is</u> for sale.

Remember that in formal writing, the verb in *there is/there are* sentences agrees
with the following noun:

   j.   There <u>is</u> a brick <u>house</u> down the street.

   k.   There <u>are</u> three <u>skylights</u> in that house.

Remember, also, that subjects containing *each, every, none,* and *no one* take singular verbs (even if the meaning of the sentence is plural):

   l.   <u>Every</u> house on the block <u>is</u> for sale.

   m.   <u>Each</u> of the houses <u>has</u> some interesting features.

   n.   <u>None</u> of them <u>is</u> cheap.

   o.   <u>No one has</u> bought one yet.

Exercise A   *Fill in the blanks with the proper form of the verb given in parentheses. Pay attention*
to tense as well as form.

Ex: 1.   On each side of the door, there ____<u>is</u>____ (be) a large potted plant.
Ex: 2.   The Japanese house, for hundreds of years, ____<u>was</u>____ (be) built of wood,
             paper, and stone.

   3.   There _____ (be) a difference between mid-twentieth-century architec-
        ture, which _____ (be) often severe and "cold," and contemporary
        architecture, which _____ (be) returning to the idea that architecture
        should be decorative. To give one example, in the middle years of this
        century, most buildings _____ (be) based on the straight line. There
        _____ (be) almost no curves in the classic skyscraper. Every line
        _____ (be) either vertical or horizontal. In recent years, however, many
        architects _____ (have) started using the curve again, for example,
        arches and rounded corners.

   4.   One of the most striking things about many American neighborhoods
        _____ (be) the variety of architectural styles. This variety _____
        (appeal) to some people, whereas others _____ (prefer) a more con-
        sistent architectural style.

   5.   Traditionally, the average American _____ (have) tried to buy his or
        her own home. Most Americans still _____ (want) to be homeowners.
        However, this _____ (have) become more difficult in recent years. The
        high cost of labor and materials _____ (be) one of the things that

_____ (have) made it so difficult to buy a home. The other factor _____ (be) high interest rates for loans.

Exercise B *Correct errors in singular/plural usage in the following essay. Some of the errors are errors of subject-verb agreement but more are noun errors, often due to confusion concerning which nouns are count and which are noncount.*

THE TRADITIONAL JAPANESE HOUSE

Ex: The traditional Japanese house has a steep roof, which is covered with tiles. The outside ~~wall~~ *walls* are made of ~~muds~~ *mud*, which ~~are~~ *is* painted white. Inside the construction is based on wood and papers. The floors is wood and are covered with tatami mat, which are made of woven straws. The inner wall are made of *shoji*, which are a kind of sliding door made of wood frames and papers. Most of these houses also have a private shrine, or altar, called *tokonoma*. In some houses you can still see the large open fireplace used for cookings, but now these are disappearing from most house.

To understand the traditional Japanese house, the most important thing to consider is the climates in Japan. In Japan the air is much more humid than in European country or in most part of the United States. That is why our houses are made from woods, papers, and tatami mats: They absorb the humidities. Also, the steep tile roof is suited for the heavy rain we have in Japan. This kind of roof is also good because we have a lot of snows in winter. The paper window and wall are also practical as well as beautiful. They allow the sunshine to come into the house and when it is hot and humid they can all be opened to let the airs circulate in the house.

ADDITIONAL WRITING TOPICS

1. Describe a famous building in your country and explain why it is so well-known.
2. Describe a traditional house in your country. Explain why this type of house is particularly suited to your country. Consider such things as climate and cultural values.
3. Design and describe an apartment complex for single people *or* one for families. Consider the needs and interests of the people who would be living in it. Justify your design.
4. Design, describe, and explain a small community of the future. It could be in the desert, on the moon, underwater, or anywhere.
5. Describe a natural scene. Be formal and exact; in other words, be precise about where things are in relation to one another.
6. Describe a *simple* piece of equipment such as a microscope, a telescope, a bicycle, a construction crane, or a camera. Describe this object very precisely, as if your reader had never seen one before. Concentrate on the structure of the object, not on how it works.

Lesson 5

PARAPHRASING AND EXPLAINING A PROCESS

Subject: Physiology and Biology

Contents:

INTRODUCTION

This lesson, and the ones that follow, are different from the first four in an important way. The writing topics in the first four lessons were based on your own experience, knowledge, or imagination. The topics were personal; you were writing about your own ideas. From now on the topics will be more academic, that is, impersonal, based on external sources of information: readings, drawings, and data.

This lesson focuses on how to gather information from a reading and then write a process essay, an essay that tells how something functions or how something is done.

Cycle One deals with the functioning of the human heart. You will learn the basic steps in the circulation of blood from a picture and then read an essay for additional information. You will see how this information could be combined in a short essay.

The topic in Cycle Two is *in vitro fertilization,* the process by which a human egg can be fertilized in a laboratory. You will learn about this process from a reading, on which you will take notes. Working from these notes, you will write a paraphrase of the reading, that is, express the main points in somewhat different language.

Adding On again emphasizes gathering information from readings, providing notetaking and paraphrase exercises, one on the human stomach, the other on a laboratory experiment. A few more specific grammar points are also introduced or reviewed in this section.

CYCLE ONE

Practice 1. Preparation: Using a Diagram

A reading on a topic such as the human heart is usually accompanied by a diagram. A reading is often easier to understand if you take the time to examine the diagram before you begin. From Figure 5-1 you can learn the general structure of the heart, the path the blood follows through the heart, and the specialized vocabulary that is used for the parts of the heart. The purpose of the two following exercises is to make sure you have extracted all this information from the diagram.

Exercise A   *The numbered vocabulary corresponds to the different parts of the heart. The vocabulary is also accompanied by a legend; for example, the term* vena cava *is followed by a box filled in with checks. To become familiar with this vocabulary, fill in the parts of the heart, using the symbols in the legend. As an example, the vena cava have been filled in with checks.*

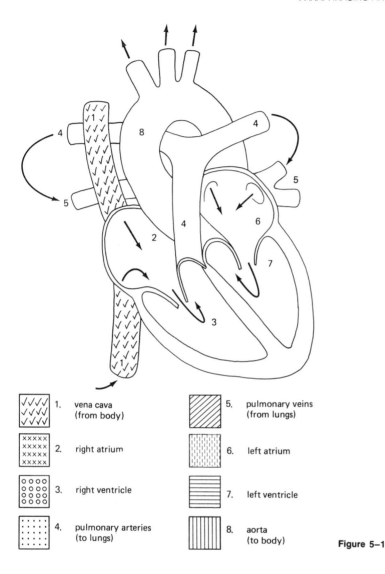

	1.	vena cava (from body)		5.	pulmonary veins (from lungs)
2.	right atrium		6.	left atrium
3.	right ventricle		7.	left ventricle
4.	pulmonary arteries (to lungs)		8.	aorta (to body)

Figure 5–1

Exercise B   *The numbers and especially the arrows in the diagram indicate the path the blood follows through the heart.*

Following the arrows in the diagram, fill in the blanks in the short outline. When you finish you will have the steps in the circulation of blood in note form, that is, in *short* written form:

Ex: 1. from the vena cava

2. to <u>the right atrium</u>

3. from the right atrium to _____
4. from the right ventricle to _____
   through the pulmonary arteries
5. from the lungs to _____
   through _____
6. from the left atrium to _____
7. from the left ventricle to the body
   through the _____

Practice 2. Reading for Information I

You now have some basic information concerning the heart: the names of the different parts of the heart and the path the blood follow through the heart. But you do not have a very clear idea concerning what the purpose of the whole process is, how the different parts of the heart function, or what the physical properties of the different parts of the heart are. If you were writing an essay on the heart, you would want to be able to describe the different parts of the heart and explain their functions.

The following reading contains such information. But it also contains information that you already know from working with the diagram. Your job as an academic reader and writer would be to take notes on the information that you need, the information that is new to you.

Exercise A   *Complete the notes that follow this reading. The notes concern the description and the function of the different parts of the heart. Notice that notes should be as short as possible, usually not complete sentences.*

THE OXYGENATION OF BLOOD

1   One of the functions of the circulatory system is to provide oxygen to the body cells. The heart receives deoxygenated, or oxygen-poor, blood from the body and pumps it to the lungs. The blood receives fresh oxygen in the lungs and is then returned to the heart, which pumps the
5   oxygenated blood back out to the body.

The Chambers of the Heart

The heart consists of four major sections, called *chambers:* the *right* and *left atria* and the *right* and *left ventricles.* The atria are thin-walled, expandable receiving chambers. The right atrium receives the
10   deoxygenated blood from the body, and the left atrium receives the bright red oxygenated blood when it returns from the lungs. The blood passes from the atria to the lower chambers, the ventricles, which are thick-walled, muscular pumps. The right ventricle pumps the oxygen-poor blood to the lungs; the left ventricle pumps the oxygen-rich blood
15   out to the body. The walls of the left ventricle are almost half an inch thick, about three times thicker than the walls of the right ventricle,

because of the strength required to pump the blood through the entire body.

The Connecting Veins and Arteries

20   Deoxygenated blood enters the right atrium of the heart through two large veins, the *vena cava*. The *superior vena cava* brings blood from the upper portion of the body, and the *inferior vena cava* carries blood from the lower part of the body. From the right atrium the blood passes into the right ventricle, which pumps it through the *pulmo-*

25 *nary arteries* to the lungs. The oxygenated blood returns to the left atrium by means of two *pulmonary veins*. The blood then passes to the left ventricle, which pumps it out to the body through an artery called the *aorta*. The aorta, the largest blood vessel in the body, may be an inch or more in diameter in adults.

Reading Notes

		Description	Function
Ex:	circulatory system		oxygenation of blood
Ex:	right atrium	thin walls, expands	
	left atrium		
	right ventricle		
	left ventricle		
	superior vena cava		
	inferior vena cava		
	pulmonary veins and arteries		
	aorta		

Exercise B   *You now have information describing the different parts of the heart and their functions. You also know the path blood follows through the heart, that is, the sequence of steps involved in the oxygenation of blood. In this exercise you have a choice. You can either write a short essay of your own on the heart (using the diagram and your reading notes) or you may prefer to complete the following essay (using your reading notes). The blanks should be filled in with physical description or functional explana- tion, as indicated by the words in parentheses. This descriptive and explanatory information can be fit into the sentences by means of nonrestrictive adjective clauses and appositives (Lesson 3, Practices 2 and 5).*

HOW THE HEART WORKS

The heart receives oxygen-poor blood from the body and pumps it to the
(or) which provide oxygen.
lungs, where it receives oxygen. The oxygen-rich blood returns to the heart,

Ex: 1.   (function)
which pumps it back out to the body.

Ex: 2.   (function)

The blood enters the heart through two large veins, the superior vena

3,4. cava, _____, and the inferior vena cava, _____. This
                (function)   (function)

5. blood enters the right atrium, _____, from which
                               (description)

6. it passes to the right ventricle. The right ventricle, _____, pumps
                                      (description)

the blood to the lungs, where it is oxygenated. The blood returns to the left

7. atrium, from which it passes to the left ventricle, _____. The left
                                      (description)

8. ventricle pumps the blood back out to the body through the aorta, _____
                                                              (description)

_____.

CYCLE TWO

Practice 3. Reading for Information II

Read the essay once or twice and answer the questions which follow. (You will use these answers again in Practice 4.) Then return to the reading, and beginning with the second paragraph, identify the steps in the process described. You might want to underline a few key words to remind you of each step and write the number of the step in the margin. (You will refer to these steps again in Practice 5.) The first two steps are done as examples.

IN VITRO FERTILIZATION

1   The process of <u>in vitro fertilization</u>, which is sometimes referred to as "test tube pregnancy," has made it possible for women with certain types of reproductive problems to become pregnant and give birth. In this process, eggs are removed from the woman's ovary and placed in labora-

5   tory dishes, where they are fertilized by sperm from her husband. Three to six days later one of the fertilized eggs is implanted in the woman's uterus, where it develops into a normal fetus.

Ex: <u>step 1</u>   The procedure begins when a <u>drug</u> is <u>administered</u> to stimulate the
Ex: <u>step 2</u>   production of eggs so the doctor will be able to remove several at once.

10   After about two weeks the eggs should be mature and the woman enters a hospital, where a minor <u>operation</u> is performed to <u>extract the eggs</u>.

        In this operation, a small cut is made in the woman's abdomen and a laparoscope is inserted. A laparoscope is a tube with a light at one end and an eyepiece at the other. This instrument, which is something like a

15   microscope with a tiny flashlight at the end, is used to search for the ripe eggs. When the mature eggs have been found, a very thin suction tube and needle are inserted into the ovary to extract the eggs. A nurse or another doctor carefully removes the eggs by sucking on the tube.

20

25

The eggs are placed in dishes with a nutrient solution to keep them alive. Sperm from the woman's husband is placed in the dishes. The fertilized eggs are kept in the nutrient solution while they begin to grow by means of cell division. When one of the eggs has divided to the eight- or sixteen-cell stage, it is transferred to the mother's uterus through another thin tube. If all goes well, the embryo (the fertilized egg) will attach to the lining of the uterus, where it will continue to grow until birth.

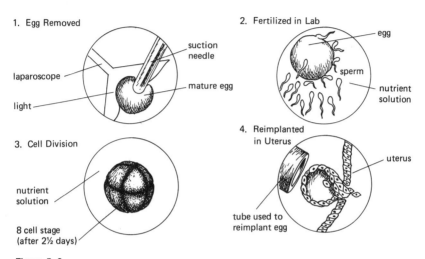

Figure 5–2

Questions
Answer these questions with short written notes. Notes do not have to be complete sentences. They should be just long enough for you to remember what they mean when you look at them later. You may want to use these notes when you get to the next exercise.

Ex: 1. When is *in vitro fertilization* necessary?
<u>reproductive problems</u> (or) <u>unable to have children</u>
2. Why is the woman given a drug two or three weeks before the operation?
3. What is a laparoscope? What is it used for?
4. How are the eggs removed from the ovary?
5. How are the eggs fertilized?
6. When is the fertilized egg put into the uterus?

Practice 4. Paraphrase and Notetaking

Paraphrase, which will be practiced several times in this lesson, is a crucial skill in academic writing, which is usually based on reading, that is, on someone else's ideas. Except for a certain amount of direct quotation, you *must not* copy from a reading: You must *paraphrase* the information you wish to use. You must, in other words, express the information in your own way, in your own words.

Students whose native language is not English often hesitate to change another writer's words because something that is published in a book or journal is certainly in good English. Why risk making errors by expressing the idea in your own words? The answer is that you will never fail because of a few grammar errors in something you write, but you may fail for copying. To repeat: Copying may be permitted, or expected, in some countries, but it is not allowed in English-speaking countries.

One way to force yourself to use paraphrase is to work from short notes rather than from the original text. Working from short notes, you will probably not remember the exact words in the original and so will have to express the idea in your own words. One of the questions following the reading, for example, is "When is *in vitro fertilization* necessary?" In short note form, this question could have been answered: *reproductive problems* or maybe *unable to have children*. If you were asked to write a complete sentence to answer the question now without looking back to the reading, you might write something like this:

a. Some women who are unable to have children can become pregnant by means of in vitro fertilization.

You would be able to write a paraphrase such as this because you would probably have forgotten that the original wording was

b. The process of in vitro fertilization has made it possible for women with certain types of reproductive problems to become pregnant.

In these examples, notice that some of the wording is not changed. The technical expression *in vitro fertilization* is not changed, nor is the word *pregnant*—what other word is there?

Of course it is possible to write paraphrase without taking notes, and in fact you probably do not take notes on most of your reading. Most students underline their text books. But working from notes is probably a good technique to use for a while, until you become quite familiar with the idea of paraphrasing. Be sure, however, you understand what your notes mean; there is no point to expressing an idea in your own words unless you have understood the idea correctly.

Exercise   *Using the short notes you took, write complete answers to the questions following the reading in Practice 3. Try to do this without looking back to the original (provided that you understand what your notes mean). An example would be sentence a above, which corresponds to question 1 on page 87. When you have finished, compare the sentences you have written with the original.*

2.
3.
4.
5.
6.

Practice 5. Directed Writing: *In Vitro Fertilization*

When you were working on the reading, you noted what the steps in the process of *in vitro fertilization* were. In this exercise you are going to paraphrase this information. You are going to explain the process of *in vitro fertilization* in your own words.

Before you begin writing, make a list—in short note form—of the steps in the process. Then, working from your notes, write one or two paragraphs explaining the process. Assume you are writing for the general reader, one who would not understand what a "laparoscope" is without some explanation. (If you were writing this for an essay exam in biology you would not have to define such terms.)

Steps

Ex: 1. drug, eggs
2. cut, laparoscope, find eggs
Continue: How is this done? What is done with the eggs, and so on?

Note: Begin with an introductory sentence or short paragraph which will tell in a general way what *in vitro fertilization* is and why it is important.

ADDING ON

Practice 6. Step Signals

Some of the time signals (Lesson 2, Practice 7) and list signals (Lesson 4, Practice 7) that you have already studied can be used to make the steps in a process clear. In this connection they might be called *step signals*. These signals, like the others, may be divided into two groups, *combining* and *noncombining*.

Some of the expressions commonly used as step signals are

Combining: when, as soon as, once, while, as, before, after, until
Noncombining: first, second . . . finally
then, next, after that

Combining signals join clauses but noncombining signals do not. The punctuation is therefore different:

  a.   <u>After</u> a mature egg is removed from the ovary, it is placed in a nutrient solution.

  b.   A mature egg is removed. Then it is placed in a nutrient solution.

  (Or)   A mature egg is removed; then it is placed in a nutrient solution.

Remember, also, that noncombining signals do not have to take the first position in a clause:

  c.   An egg is removed. <u>Next</u> it is placed in a nutrient solution.

  (Or)   An egg is removed. It is <u>next</u> placed in a nutrient solution.

Exercise   *Fill in the blanks in the following sentences with step signals. The punctuation and the position of the blanks in the sentences will make it clear whether you need a combining or a noncombining expression. In some cases there may be more than one possible correct answer.*

Ex: 1.   The process of *in vitro fertilization* begins a couple of weeks before the woman enters the hospital. She is __first__ given a drug to increase the production of eggs.

Ex: 2.   She checks into a hospital a couple of weeks later __when__ the eggs are mature.

   3.   A small cut is made in the woman's abdomen; _____ a laparoscope is inserted.

   4.   _____ the doctor can see the eggs through the laparoscope, he or she carefully inserts a suction needle into the ovary.

   5.   _____ the first doctor holds the needle in place, a nurse, or a second doctor, slowly sucks the eggs into a suction tube.

   6.   The eggs are _____ transferred from the suction tube to a nutrient solution.

   7.   Fertilization is possible _____ the sperm have been added to the dish.

   8.   The fertilized egg is carefully observed _____ it begins to divide.

   9.   First, the egg divides into two, four, eight, and _____ sixteen cells.

   10.   _____ the egg has reached the sixteen-cell stage, it is implanted in the uterus.

Practice 7. Paraphrase and Summary

Your paraphrase of the reading on *in vitro fertilization* was probably shorter than the original; if so it was a summary. In the simplest sense a summary is just a short paraphrase. The difficulty is knowing which information to include and which to leave out. Consider the following information on the stomach:

   a.   One of the major functions of the stomach is to mix food with gastric secretions, which break down the food molecules, until a semi-fluid mass of partly digested food called <u>chyme,</u> Greek word for juice, is formed.

Probably everyone would agree that the least important information in this sentence is the phrase *Greek word for juice.* You might feel that the most important information could be written down in note form as follows:

   b.   1 function: food + gastric secretions → semi-fluid

Working from these notes your paraphrase (or summary) might be

   c.   One of the functions of the stomach is mixing food with gastric secretions until it becomes semi-fluid.

This paraphrase/summary is about half the length of the original. Note-taking, as you have seen, is a good way to approach paraphrase because when working from notes you will naturally use your own language except for certain basic vocabulary and technical terms. Notetaking is also an excellent way to approach summary because it forces you to concentrate on the main ideas, to extract the most important information.

Exercise   *Write a one-, or at most two-, paragraph summary of the following reading. Begin by underlining the most important information and then take notes on this underlined information. Work from your notes. Note: In a summary it is often possible to change the order or the organization of the information. The following reading, for example, begins by describing the functions of the stomach and then describes its structure; you would not have to do it in this order.*

THE STOMACH*

1   *What is the Nature of the Stomach?*
        The *stomach* is the most widened or enlarged portion of the digestive tube. It is located just below the diaphragm on the left side of the body. Its three major functions are to store food; to mix food with gastric secretions
5   until the semi-fluid mass of partly digested food called *chyme*, Greek word for juice, is formed; and to permit the chyme to slowly empty into the duodenum at a rate suitable for proper digestion and absorption by the small intestine.
        When empty, the stomach is only about the size of a large sausage.

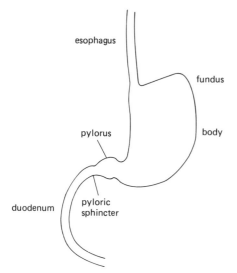

Figure 5–3

*From Stanley W. Jacob and Clarice Ashwort Francone, *Elements of Anatomy and Physiology* (Philadelphia: W. B. Saunders Co., 1976), pp. 159–163.

10   After a meal, however, it expands considerably. There are three parts or
sections to the stomach: the *fundus,* an upper portion ballooning to the left
side of the body; the *body* or central portion; and the *pylorus,* a relatively
narrowed portion at the end of the stomach just before the entrance into the
duodenum (small intestine). The term "pylorus" is from the Greek word for
15   gatekeeper. At the very end of the pylorus is the *pyloric sphincter,* which
opens and closes at appropriate times to allow the flow of chyme into the
duodenum. The term "sphincter" always refers to a muscle that closes off
some hollow tube or chamber.

The walls of the stomach have an extra layer of muscular tissue not
20   found in other areas of the digestive tube. With its *three* layers of smooth
muscle, the stomach is one of the strongest organs of the body. It is well
suited to the task of mechanically breaking up food through its strong
churning actions. This churning also serves to mix the tiny food particles
thoroughly with the gastric juice.

25   The gastric juices, which begin the chemical breakdown of the food
molecules, are secreted by the thousands of microscopic gland cells located
in the inner lining of the stomach wall. Hydrochloric acid, HCL, is one of
the more important and effective digestive substances making up the gastric
juices.

Practice 8. The Past Passive

In the reading on *in vitro fertilization* you may have noticed that many of the verbs
were in the passive voice. *What* is done in this process is more important than *who*

does it. The verbs were in the present passive because the steps in the process are usually more or less the same.

If you were reporting on something done in the past, however, rather than focusing on the fact that the process is always the same, you would use the past passive. If, for example, you had witnessed the procedures involved in *in vitro fertilization* and were writing about what you saw, you might write:

a. A suction tube <u>was put</u> into the ovary and the eggs <u>were</u> <u>extracted.</u>

Exercise   *One writing situation in which you would use the past passive would be a lab report. The important thing is what was done, not who did it. (The teacher knows very well that you are the one who did it.)*

The following experiment measures the effect of light on the rate of photosynthesis. Photosynthesis is the process by which green plants transform the energy of sunlight into glucose, a carbohydrate. One of the things necessary for photosynthesis to take place is light. One of the products of the process is oxygen, which the plant releases into the atmosphere. In this experiment the amount of light shining on a plant is varied and the amount of oxygen released is measured. The purpose is to see if increasing the amount of light increases the amount of oxygen released, to see, in other words, if a greater amount of light increases the rate of photosynthesis.

You are given instructions from a laboratory manual. Imagine you have already performed the experiment. (You are also given sample data.) Write a laboratory report telling what was done and what the results were.

You will not need to use all the information in the instructions in your report. For example, the first instruction is "Obtain a piece of the plant Elodea *from the instructor. Place it in a test tube." In your report you would not have to tell where you got the plant, but you would want to say what you did with it. You might write, "A piece of* Elodea *was placed in a test tube."*

In other words, summarize the instructions in writing your report. At each step ask yourself how much of the information given should be included in your report. Use the past passive. It would probably be best to work from notes again.

THE EFFECT OF LIGHT ON PHOTOSYNTHETIC RATE[*]

Ex: 1. Obtain a piece of the plant *Elodea* from the instructor. Place it in a test tube. Note: <u>*Elodea*, test tube.</u>

2. Fill the tube with 0.5% $NaHCO_3$ (sodium bicarbonate). (Note: The sodium bicarbonate acts as an extra source of CO_2 [carbon dioxide], which is one of the things necessary for photosynthesis to take place.)

3. Place the tube in a rack, 50 cm from a lamp with a 75-watt bulb.

*Adapted from LAB MANUAL TO ACCOMPANY *EXPLORING BIOLOGY* BY PAMELA S. CAMP AND KAREN ARMS by Virginia Fry. Copyright (c) 1981 by CBS College Publishing. Reprinted by permission of Saunders College Publishing, CBS College Publishing.

The Heat Sink

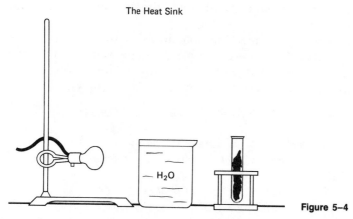

Figure 5–4

4. Place a 1000 ml beaker of water as a "heat sink" about 4 cm from the test-tube rack (Figure 5-4).
   (Note: The heat sink allows light to pass through but absorbs heat so that the only variable in this experiment will be the quantity of light.)

5. Turn on the light. Wait until bubbles of oxygen begin rising regularly. Count the number of bubbles produced in a three-minute period.
   (Note: The verbs *wait* and *begin rising* cannot be made passive here.)

6. Repeat for another three-minute period and calculate the average number of bubbles.

7. Record the average number of oxygen bubbles produced in three minutes on the graph below (Figure 5-5).

Figure 5–5

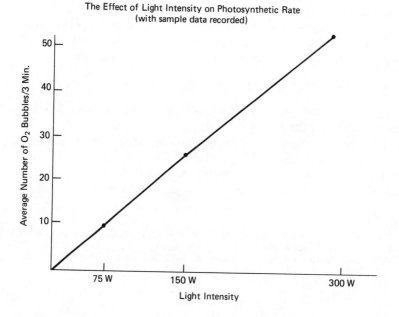

The Effect of Light Intensity on Photosynthetic Rate
(with sample data recorded)

8. Repeat the procedure twice, first with a 150-watt bulb, then with a 300-watt bulb. Add fresh water and sodium bicarbonate to the test tube each time. (Note: Sample data have been provided in figure 5-5.)

Practice 9. Reviewing Definition

You have seen the importance of defining any terms that may not be clear to a reader. Such definition is especially common in scientific or technical writing, which always aims to explain something unfamiliar. Three of the patterns already studied (Lesson 3, Practices 2 and 8) are quite useful in scientific writing:

a. The atria, which are the upper chambers of the heart, are reservoirs.
　　　　　　　　　　(nonrestrictive adjective clause)
b. The atria, the upper chambers of the heart, are reservoirs.
　　　　　　　　　(appositive)
c. The atria, that is, the upper chambers of the heart, are reservoirs.
　　　　(restatement signal)

The word *or* is also used as a restatement signal in formal writing:

d. The atria, *or* the upper chambers of the heart, are reservoirs.

In all these examples the term to be defined (atria) precedes the definition (the upper chambers of the heart). In the following example notice that this order is reversed:

e. The upper chambers of the heart, called (or named) atria, are reservoirs.

Exercise *Combine the following pairs of sentences as indicated by the words in parentheses. The information in the second sentence will define the italicized term in the first sentence.*

Ex: 1. Light enters the eye through the *cornea.* The cornea is a transparent tissue covering the front of the eyeball. (which)
Light enters the eye through the cornea, <u>which is a transparent tissue covering the front of the eyeball.</u>

2. The space behind the cornea is filled with a *watery liquid.* The watery liquid is the aqueous humor. (called)

3. The *aqueous humor* lies behind the cornea. It is a watery liquid. (that is)

4. Behind the aqueous humor is the *iris.* The iris is a ring of tissue that opens and contracts allowing light to enter. (appositive)

5. The *iris* determines eye color. The iris is pigmented tissue. (which)

6. This *pigmented* tissue determines eye color. Pigmented means colored. (or)

7. The muscles in the iris open and close the *pupil.* The pupil is the dark hole in the center of the eye. (appositive)

8. The light passes through the pupil to the *lens.* The lens focuses the image. (which)

9. After being focused, the light passes through the eyeball to the *retina.* The retina is the inner surface of the eye. (that is)

10. A *nerve* transmits an image from the retina to the brain. It is the optic nerve. (named)

Practice 10. Proofreading

Exercise   *Correct any errors you may find in the following essay.*

FLOWER ARRANGING: A TRADITIONAL JAPANESE ART

Many Japanese study the traditional art of flower arranging.

                                                                     is
Ex: The basic style of flower arranging|called *moribana*.

                     are   a   is
Ex: To do *moribana*, three things|necessary:|shallow bowl, which|square, round, or oval in shape, a stem holder and a flower scissors.

There are three basic lines, or flowers, in *moribana: shu* which represent heaven, *fuku* represent man and *kyaku* represent earth. Here is a drawing of their proper arrangement:

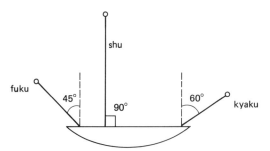

Figure 5–6

First, *shu*, which is the main flower, has to be place in the rear left of the container at 90° angle. *Shu* has to be 1½ to 2 time higher than the wide of the bowl. *Fuku*, second line, is place in front of and to the left of *shu*. It lean over the side of the bowl at 45° angle. It should ⅔ the high of *shu*. Next, *kyaku* is placed in the front right of bowl lean over the edge at 60° angle.

When these basic line are in place, two more flower is added to balance the arrangement. These flower are called *helper*. One is place between *shu* and *fuku*. Other is place between *shu* and *kyaku*. Here what the finish arrangement look like:

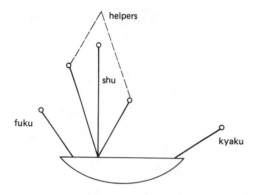

Figure 5–7

ADDITIONAL WRITING TOPICS

1. Using paraphrase, explain a process that you have read about. The process could be from almost any field: science, social science, engineering, business, and so on. Turn in with the essay a photocopy of the reading you have used.

2. Write a lab report of an experiment, either one you have done or one you have read about. Keep in mind that you are writing this report for an English teacher: Be sure your explanation is clear. If you use directions from a laboratory workbook, turn in a photocopy of the directions with your report—which should be in your own English.

3. From your own knowledge, explain how something is done. Choose something which is not common knowledge. Do not, for example, explain how to make a sandwich or wash a car. Interesting topics might be such things as a traditional art, craft, or game from your country or an interesting skill or hobby.

Lesson Six

DIVIDING INFORMATION

Subject: Computer Applications

Contents:

—Reading
—Dividing Information Effectively
—The Topic Sentence
—Directed Writing: Computer Applications in the Home
—Parallelism
—The Introductory Paragraph and the Thesis Statement
—Relevance and the Topic Sentence
—Formal Classification
—Sentences of Division and Classification
—Proofreading: Modals

INTRODUCTION

The ability to divide information into meaningful groups is extremely important both as a way to organize an essay and, more generally, as a way to focus thinking. We can simplify complex subjects by dividing them into parts; and once we have simplified or ordered them in this way, we can write about them clearly. The question of the division of information has been touched on earlier in this book (in Lessons 1 and 2), but in this lesson the logic of division is examined in much greater detail. The use of generalization, especially topic sentences, is also thoroughly reviewed.

Cycle One begins with a reading that divides the applications of computers in education into three major groups. The logic involved in such a division is analyzed and the use of general ideas (topic sentences) to group information is reviewed.

In Cycle Two you are presented with a variety of computer applications in the home. Your task is to find a logical way to divide these computer functions into groups and then write an essay based on this division.

Adding On introduces important new organizational and logical questions. A very common type of introductory paragraph is presented, and the special problems connected with formal classification, the most rigorous type of logical division, are considered.

CYCLE ONE

Practice 1. Reading

COMPUTERS IN EDUCATION

1

Computers have begun to affect education just as they have affected almost every aspect of modern life. Indeed they may be especially suited to instructional use because they are tireless, patient, and responsive to the needs of the individual learner. The number of possible applications of computers to education is enormous but most programs are built on a few basic approaches to teaching. In fact, instructional programs can be divided into three main groups according to their primary method of instruction: tutorial, drill and practice, or simulation.

5

10

The tutorial function is the one which introduces and explains new concepts or information. In other words, a tutorial program teaches, in the most common sense of the word. A tutorial program, for instance, might present the basic content of a course in psychology or physics. Typically, such programs present and explain something new and then test the student to see if it has been learned. If a student is having trouble understanding an idea, the tutorial program will explain it again, in a different way.

15

As all teachers and students know, however, learning requires more than explanation. Drill and practice programs, as the name indi-
20 cates, provide the repetition necessary to master new skills and concepts. Such programs are especially useful in teaching subjects which require a great deal of practice: arithmetic, spelling, grammar, typing. The ability of the computer to individualize practice makes drill and practice pro- grams especially useful. This kind of program can keep track of the
25 points which are difficult for a particular student and give him or her extra practice on just these points.

The third major application of computers in education is in creating simulations. A simulation program presents the student with a real life situation in which various problems arise. The student must
30 react to the situation and analyze and solve the problems. Business stu- dents, for example, might work with a simulated corporate situation, deciding, perhaps, how much to produce, how much to charge, how much to buy or sell. Medical students might practice diagnosing and treating imaginary patients with imaginary symptoms. Simulations are
35 especially valuable because they give the student immediate feedback on his or her decisions, showing what the real life consequences of various actions would be.

Questions

1. What are the three main computer functions in educational programs?
2. Which sentence in the essay indicates that the essay is going to discuss these three functions?
3. What is a tutorial program?
4. Which sentence expresses the main idea of the second paragraph?
5. What is the difference between a tutorial program and a drill and practice program?
6. What is the topic of the third paragraph? Of the fourth paragraph?
7. What is a simulation?
8. Does this essay contain any "paragraph bridges" (Lesson 2, Practice 6)?

Practice 2. Dividing Information Effectively

To divide information into logical groups, you must first see whether things which seem different, or unrelated, might in fact have something in common. At first a computer program which requires a student to make decisions about buying and selling stocks seems very different from one which requires a medi- cal student to decide which medicine to give an imaginary patient. But they both ask the student to make decisions about realistic problems in an imaginary situa- tion. So they can be grouped together as simulations. Simulation is a general idea which can be used to group together a variety of different specifics. In an essay these specifics become examples supporting the general idea.

There are several problems to keep in mind when dividing information. In a good division the categories will be *distinct, balanced,* and *limited.*

First, the general ideas you use must truly separate the information into two or more groups. The groups must be distinct. You could not, for example, divide the uses of computers in education into learning programs and drill and practice programs: drill and practice is one kind of learning. The division would not be *distinct*. (See Figure 6-1.)

Figure 6–1

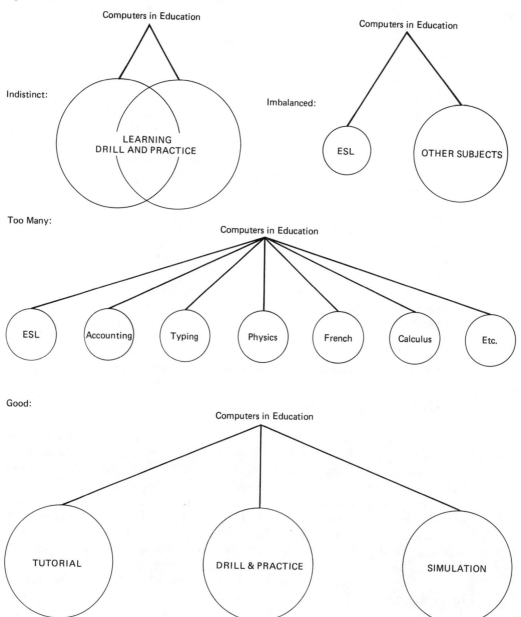

Second, a good division is one which divides information into equally general groups, or *balanced* categories. Obviously, you would not say that the two main uses of computers in education are teaching ESL and teaching other subjects. One category would contain only one subject, whereas the other might contain a hundred. One would be too specific, the other too general. The division would not be *balanced*. (See Figure 6-1.)

Third, it is better to divide into a few general groups rather than into many specific ones. How many groups would result if the educational uses of computers were divided according to subject matter: accounting, typing, physics, French, calculus, and so on? There would be too many categories. The division would not be *limited*. (See Figure 6-1.)

Exercise A *The following list gives several possible applications of computers to ESL or foreign language study. Divide this list according to the ideas we have been using: tutorial, drill and practice, simulation. See the example which follows the list.*

1. Explain a new grammar rule.
2. Provide a grammar review exercise.
3. Produce an individualized spelling exercise.
4. Take the role of a salesperson in a "conversation."
5. Provide pictures (computer graphics) to make the meaning of vocabulary clear.
6. Generate reading passages which automatically become more difficult as the student progresses.
7. Use graphics and "conversation" to create an arrival in a foreign city: airport, taxi, hotel.
8. Give examples of paraphrase.

Tutorial	**Drill and Practice**	**Simulation**
Ex: 1. new rule	2. review exercise	

Exercise B *The following list concerns some of the uses of computers in a modern business. Divide this list into two categories. One of the categories is given at the end of the list. What could the other category logically be? See examples.*

1. Do automatic billing.
2. Forecast sales.
3. Make video conferences possible.
4. Do word processing.
5. Do payroll automatically.
6. Provide data such as sales reports.
7. Estimate cost of project.

Aid to Office Workers	_____?
Ex: 1. automatic billing	2. forecast sales

Exercise C   Divide the following list of computer applications in hospitals into two groups; that is, find two general ideas that can be used to divide this information.

1. Aid doctors in diagnosing illness.
2. Suggest possible treatment or medication.
3. Prepare hospital bills.
4. Automatically reorder supplies.
5. Remind nurses of patients' medication schedules.
6. Keep personnel records.
7. Interpret laboratory test results.
8. Analyze hospital efficiency and suggest ways to lower costs.

Exercise D   In this exercise you are given some possible divisions of the information in Exercises B (business applications) and C (medical applications). In the blank following the division write good, not distinct, not balanced, or not limited. Note: A bad division may be bad in more than one way; it might, for example, be both indistinct and unbalanced.

Ex:	1.	business:	do routine jobs, aid in decision making	good
	2.	business:	do routine jobs, help in sales	not balanced
	3.	business:	secretaries, receptionists, clerks, supervisors, executives	_____
	4.	business:	help management, help employees	_____
	5.	business:	help office workers, help secretaries	_____
	6.	hospital:	patient care, administration	_____
	7.	hospital:	medical, patient care	_____

Practice 3. The Topic Sentence

The kinds of division you have been practicing suggest an obvious kind of essay organization: The parts of the essay will correspond to the categories in the division. A long essay on the use of computers in hospitals, for example, might be divided into two main sections: medical applications and administrative applications. A short essay would have the same basic structure but might devote just one paragraph to each of these divisions. The introductory reading provides a similar example. In the first paragraph three types of educational computer programs are mentioned: tutorial, drill and practice, and simulation. In the rest of the essay one paragraph is devoted to explaining in more detail each of these main functions.

The second paragraph, for example, develops the idea of tutorial programs, and this intention is stated in the first sentence of the paragraph: *A tutorial program is one which introduces and explains a new concept.* A sentence like this one, one that clearly states the main idea of a paragraph, is called a *topic sentence* (Lesson 2, Practice 3).

A topic sentence should "fit" the contents of a paragraph rather closely; in other words, it should be neither more specific nor more general than necessary to indicate the main idea or the contents of a paragraph. Neither of these two sentences, for example, would fit as the topic sentence of the second paragraph of the introductory reading:

a. Tutorial programs help students learn.

b. Tutorial programs will explain an idea over and over again.

The first sentence is too general: All educational programs help students learn. The second is too specific: This is only one feature of a tutorial program. Neither fits, or matches, the idea the paragraph will present.

Not all paragraphs have a clearly identifiable topic sentence. But when they do, it will usually—not always—be found near the beginning of the paragraph. It is often the first or second sentence of the paragraph.

When the first sentence of a paragraph is not the topic sentence, it may be functioning as a paragraph bridge (see Lesson 2, Practice 6). A paragraph bridge takes a reader from the topic which has just been concluded to the one which the new paragraph will develop. The third paragraph of the introductory reading begins with a bridge:

c. As all students and teachers know, however, learning requires more than explanation.

In this sentence the word *explanation* refers back to the topic of the preceding paragraph: tutorial programs. The next sentence introduces the new topic:

d. Drill and practice programs, as the name indicates, provide the repetition necessary to master new skills and concepts.

Exercise   *Write topic sentences for the following paragraphs.*

Ex.   1.   Students are not the only ones to benefit from computers in education. Many teachers are finding that computers can reduce their work load and improve their teaching. Computers can free teachers from certain kinds of time-consuming bookkeeping. Test items can be "banked" in a computer, greatly reducing the time required to produce a new test. Tests can be scored by computer, and more importantly, the computer can analyze the test results, indicating to the teacher which points may need further treatment in class. Classroom computers also make it possible for a teacher to give individual attention to students who are having trouble. While the rest of a class is working on an educational program, the teacher can take the time to work directly with a student who is falling behind.

2.   More and more businesses are using "electronic mail." This term refers to the transmission of information—words, data, images—directly from one

computer terminal to another. To give an example, a secretary in Houston could type a business report on his or her word processor, which would then immediately send the message to a computer in the New York office of the same company. "Voice mail" is also made possible by computer technology. In an office with "voice mail," it is not necessary to keep phoning a busy number over and over again. The phone message is electronically stored and passed on as soon as the line is free. Computer capabilities are also making "video conferences" a realistic alternative to the business trip. Using computerized video technology, executives in different cities or countries can see each other on television screens and discuss business without leaving their offices._____

3. _____

The computerized cash register, also known as a Point of Sale (POS) System, automatically controls inventory. In other words, it keeps track of exactly how many of a particular item have been sold and how many are left in stock. A POS system can also keep track of how well a new item, or one that has been advertised, is selling. It keeps a record of how much each salesperson sells. A POS system will even keep a record of which items are returned. All of this information is extremely useful to store managers.

4. _____

In many libraries the familiar card catalogs are being replaced by computer terminals. Libraries are often linked by computer so that if one library does not have a book it can be quickly determined if another does. Indeed, library computer systems are sometimes linked to national data banks, making it possible for a researcher to have access to information stored hundreds or thousands of miles away. Of course, libraries also use computers to keep records about which books are checked out, when they are due, who has them, and so on.

CYCLE TWO

Practice 4. Directed Writing: Computer Applications in the Home

Figure 6-2 shows a variety of household computer functions. Many are technologically possible now; others may be possible in the fairly near future. List these functions on a separate piece of paper and find a way to divide them into two or three main groups. Which of these functions have something in common and so can be grouped together? Do not worry if one or two of the functions do not fit into your categories, but try to make your categories balanced; that is, each one should be equally general and contain a similar number of functions. When you have divided the functions into groups, write an essay on the topic of

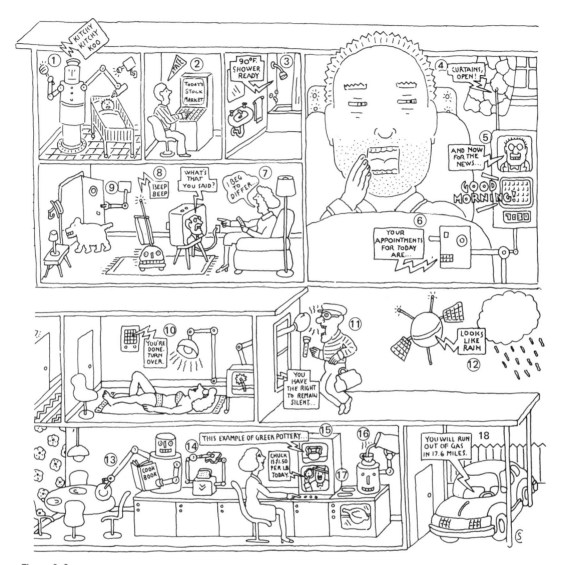

Figure 6–2

household computer applications. The following might help you organize your essay:

Introduction: Background: Make general comments on the computer revolution.
Division: Introduce in one sentence the two or three general categories you have divided the functions into. (See the last sentence in the first paragraph of the introductory reading.)

Development: Write one paragraph explaining and giving examples of each of the general categories mentioned in the introduction. You do not have to use every bit of information on your list, but give two or three examples of each general idea.

The general idea that each paragraph develops should be expressed in a clear topic sentence. You may also want to use paragraph bridges: Lead into the new topic by repeating some of the information from a previous paragraph.

Conclusion: Write brief thoughts on the home of the future.

ADDING ON

Practice 5. Parallelism

Parallelism is a general principle of style that says that ideas of equal importance, such as items in a list, or categories in a sentence of division, should be expressed in parallel grammatical structure if possible:

a. Two important functions of the home computer will be bring<u>ing</u> huge amounts of information into the home and do<u>ing</u> household chores.

Bringing and *doing* are both gerunds; they are parallel grammatical structures. The two ideas in the following example are not expressed in parallel form:

b. *Home robots might be able <u>to cook</u> and <u>housecleaning</u> is a job they could do.

This sentence could be made parallel by making both ideas infinitives (like *to cook*) as in example c or gerunds (like *housecleaning*) as in example d.:

c. Home robots might be able to <u>cook</u> and <u>clean</u> house.

d. <u>Cooking</u> and <u>housekeeping</u> are two jobs that home robots might be able to do.

These examples have used gerunds and infinitives. Any grammatical structure may used in a parallel construction. A parallel construction may involve two or more nouns, verbs, adjectives, or adjective clauses, to give just a few examples.

Exercise *Find the elements in the following sentences that should be in parallel construction and then rewrite the sentences so they are. There may be more than one correct way to do this.*

Ex: 1. Three professions in which computers are being used are education, business, and by doctors.
Three professions in which computers are being used are <u>education, business, and medicine.</u>

(or) Computers are being used professionally by <u>educators, businesspersons, and doctors.</u>

2. In the retail business computers control inventory and reordering is automatic.

3. Computers have made possible "electronic mail" and executives can meet by means of video technology.

4. In supermarkets computers give a daily sales report, take inventory, and when you pay they automatically add up your bill.

5. In the home, computers may be able to cook dinner, temperature control, or even play with the children.

6. Home computers can do unpleasant chores and the information they can give us will be useful.

7. Home computers may control the home environment by turning lights on and off, maintenance of a constant temperature, and they may even turn televisions and radios on and off automatically.

8. Computers will be useful in the kitchen doing such things as menu planning and they may even do some cooking.

Practice 6. The Introductory Paragraph and the Thesis Statement

In a formal academic essay, the introduction often consists of general background information followed by a statement of the purpose, focus, or point of the essay. This statement is sometimes called the *thesis statement* and is often the last sentence of the introduction.

The background information is usually general and already known to the reader; it leads to the thesis statement, which is more specific and states an idea or information new to the reader:

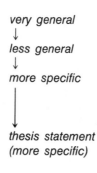

very general
↓
less general
↓
more specific
↓
thesis statement
(more specific)

In the last fifteen or twenty years, computers have begun to influence almost every area of modern life. We are accustomed to seeing computers in the workplace, in stores, and in schools and universities. It is not surprising that computers and computerized robots may some day make home life easier and more interesting. In the home, computers will do unpleasant chores, maintain an efficient and pleasant environment, and make available great amounts of information.

known
↓
new

After reading this introduction the reader will expect the essay to discuss three things: chores, home environment, and information.

As you can see, the thesis statement and the topic sentence are closely related: The one states the topic of the essay as a whole; the other states the topic of a single paragraph.

Exercise   *Choose one of the following thesis ideas concerning computer applications and write an introductory paragraph. The divisions in the thesis sentence should be in parallel grammatical form.*

1. Computers for teachers: keep records, save time in writing tests and exercises.
2. Computers in banking: automated service, record keeping.
3. Computers in architecture: design, cost prediction.
4. Computers in the office: office workers, managers.
5. Computers in the library: aid in research, keep records.

Practice 7. Relevance and the Topic Sentence

In Lesson 1 (Practice 2) you were introduced to the idea that all the information in an essay must be relevant, or related, to the purpose of the essay. In the same way, all the information in a particular paragraph must relate clearly to the main idea of the paragraph, which is often expressed in a topic sentence. Irrelevant material will confuse the reader and make the organization of the ideas unclear.

The underlined sentences in the following paragraph are off the topic, irrelevant to the main idea (which is stated in the first sentence):

> We often hear that computers are cold or inhuman, but in fact many people are more comfortable with a computer than with another person. Computers are patient and do not judge the people who use them. <u>They are fast and reliable.</u> Many students who would be embarrassed to show a teacher that they do not understand something are happy to ask a computer questions. Some patients would rather explain their health problems to a computer than to a doctor. There is even a computer program which deals with psychological problems. The program has become popular because many people are uncomfortable discussing such problems with another person. <u>The professor who wrote the program is upset that people are using this program instead of going to see a psychotherapist. His intention in writing the program was to demonstrate that computers could be programmed to have "intelligent" conversations with humans, not to replace trained therapists.</u>

It is not hard to understand how even a good writer can get off the topic. One idea will usually suggest another, but this second idea may not be relevant to the topic. We are often told, for example, that computers are patient, fast, and reliable. Their "patience" is related to the topic of this paragraph, but their speed and reliability are not. Students are not more comfortable with computers because they are fast and reliable (so are most teachers) but because they are patient (unlike some teachers).

Similarly, the information about the professor who wrote the psychology program is not relevant because it has nothing to do with why people like the program. However, such a program immediately suggests the idea of the dehumanizing effect of computers, which might be a very good topic—for another paragraph.

The mistakes in this paragraph are not foolish or ignorant, but the writer has not been strict enough concerning which information belonged in the paragraph and which did not: It must *all* be relevant.

Exercise *In the following paragraphs, underline the topic sentence and cross out any information which is not relevant. The paragraph just discussed can be used as an example: The first sentence (that people are comfortable with computers) would be underlined, and the information about the speed and reliability of computers and about the professor who wrote the psychology program would be crossed out.*

1. Computers have completely changed the accounting and bookkeeping departments of most large businesses. These departments used to have very large staffs but now are filled with computer systems. In fact in many sectors of the economy people are losing their jobs to computers. Monthly statements, invoices, and bills can be stored in computer memory, updated constantly, and printed out when needed. Computers can instantly provide managers with information on cash flow, spending, and profits. Computer systems can free us from much dull, routine work.

2.   Computer systems known as Electronic Funds Transfer (EFT) are changing the way we bank, shop, and pay bills. EFT makes it possible to withdraw or deposit money automatically or transfer money from one account to another. The most familiar example of EFT is the automatic teller machine outside most banks. It is not so widely known that in some stores it is possible to pay for merchandise by means of EFT. In such a system, a customer's bank number is entered on a computerized cash register and the amount of the sale is automatically transferred from the customer's bank account to the store's bank account. These computerized cash registers, known as Point of Sale (POS) systems, are also used to keep inventory, reorder, and update sales information. Another use of EFT is known as preauthorized banking, which makes it possible for many routine transactions to be performed automatically. A pay check, for example, might be automatically deposited or monthly bills automatically paid and the amount subtracted from a customer's account.

3.   Computers make possible a very thorough type of health examination known as the multiphasic physical. In this kind of physical the patient fills out a long questionnaire about his or her health history and the health history of close relatives. The patient then performs a variety of physical tests, gives blood and urine, and goes home. The questionnaire, the test data, and blood and urine samples are all analyzed by computer. On the basis of all this information the computer is able to bring any abnormality or possible health problem to the doctor's attention. This same ability to handle large amounts of data quickly has made the computer essential in medical research and hospital administration. The doctor evaluates the computer report, and when the patient comes for an office visit, answers any questions and orders additional tests if necessary.

4.   We may soon see the development of the "electronic newspaper," that is, news transmitted directly to a home computer terminal. A subscriber to an electronic newspaper would be able to specify what kind of news he or she is most interested in. To give an example, a person who is interested in a certain part of the world—Africa, Asia, South America—could receive much more information about that part of the world than is available in the daily newspaper or on the nightly news. In fact, foreigners living in the United States are often surprised at how narrow American news coverage is. To give another example, a person interested in science could receive much more news about scientific developments than a regular newspaper carries.

Practice 8. Formal Classification

As you have seen, logic is important in the kinds of division you have been practicing. Another kind of division, based on even stricter logic, is *formal classification*. Formal classification is different from informal division in two important ways: There must be a clear method of division, and it must account for all the data:

a. (According to what they eat,) mammals can be divided into carnivores, herbivores, and omnivores.

The method or criterion for this division is "what they eat." Three classes of mammals result from this division: meat eaters, plant eaters, and mammals that eat both. This division accounts for all the data: All mammals fall into one of these groups.

The logic in informal division is similar but not so strict. It would be difficult to state simply what the criterion of division is in this sentence:

b. Computers are important in both hospital administration and patient care.

Also, this sentence does not try to cover *all* the uses of computers in medicine. The use of computers in medical research, for example, would not fit into either of these categories.

You can see now that the problem of indistinct division which you studied earlier in the lesson is caused by mixing two different criteria of division. The division in the following sentence is not distinct, or logical, because two criteria have been used to classify mammals: what they eat and whether they are wild or not.

c. *Mammals can be divided into herbivores, wild and domestic.

You should also note that a formal criterion of division sometimes produces unequal categories. If living creatures are divided according to the element for which they are best suited, four categories result: air, land, water, and amphibious (land and water). There are fewer amphibians than land animals, for example, but this imbalance is acceptable because the criterion is logical. Clearly the same data can be classified in different ways by using different criteria of division. Cats and cows belong in the same category if classified according to domesticity; if classified according to diet, they belong to different categories.

Exercise A   The "mystery objects" in Figure 6-3 can be classified in different ways by using different criteria of division. Fill in the following blanks. Sometimes you are given the criterion and have to divide the pictures into groups; sometimes you are given the groups and must decide what criterion has been used.

		Criterion	**Class I**	**Class II**	**Class III**
Ex:	1.	Color	A, B, E	C, D	
	2.	Cost	_____	_____	
	3.	_____	A, B, D	C, E	
	4.	_____	C	_____	_____
	5.	_____	A, E	_____	_____

Exercise B   In this exercise you are asked to classify "moving objects with wheels." A few examples would be cars, trains, bicycles, toy trucks, skateboards, wheelchairs, trucks, and so on. You are given the criteria of division and have to determine what general classes will

Mystery Objects

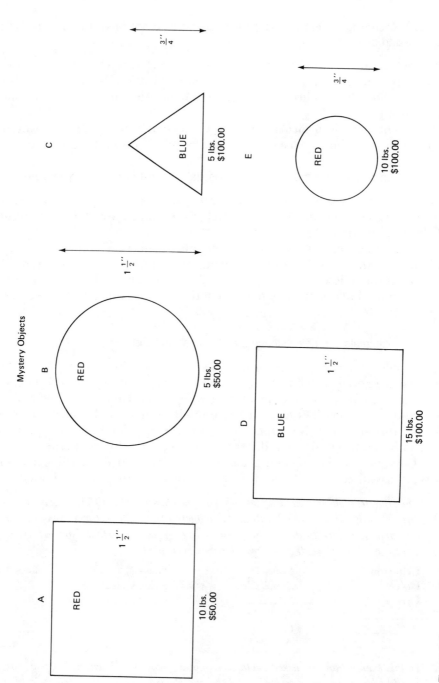

A

RED

$1\frac{1}{2}''$

10 lbs.
$50.00

B

RED

$1\frac{1}{2}''$

5 lbs.
$50.00

C

BLUE

$\frac{3}{4}''$

5 lbs.
$100.00

D

BLUE

$1\frac{1}{2}''$

15 lbs.
$100.00

E

RED

$\frac{3}{4}''$

10 lbs.
$100.00

Figure 6–3

114

result from them; also give examples of which items will fit into each of these classes. Notice that you may have to define some of the terms you use. If you divide these objects with wheels according to speed, you will probably decide that one of the resulting classes is "fast-moving" objects with wheels. But how are you defining the word "fast"?

Criterion

Ex: 1. primary purpose

recreation: skateboard, toy truck
necessity: bus, wheelchair, truck
either: bicycle

2. source of power

3. speed

4. cost

5. technological complexity

6. sport or not

Exercise C *In this exercise, decide which of the divisions are illogical because more than one criterion has been used.*

Ex: 1. cars: fast, expensive (Illogical.)
2. cars: domestic, imported (Logical.)
3. television programs: entertaining, educational, comedy
4. television programs: factual, fictional
5. modern economic systems: socialistic, capitalistic, mixed
6. modern economic systems: socialistic, capitalistic, authoritarian
7. teachers: authoritarian, democratic
8. teachers: nervous, boring

Exercise D   *In this exercise you will choose a general topic and decide how you might classify it formally. Your division should be based on a clear criterion and account for all the data included in the topic.*

In this exercise your teacher may ask you to write a paragraph based on your classification. If so, you should keep in mind that a good classification would be one that is not only logical but also fairly precise and interesting. It would be possible to divide teachers into good and bad, for example, but this is so vague that it would be hard to write about without a good deal of further definition. It might also be logical to divide teachers into calm and nervous, but it would not be very useful to you as a writer: What could you say about teachers using this division? On the other hand, dividing teachers into authoritarian and democratic might serve as the basis of an interesting paragraph. The words have fairly precise meaning, and the idea might be interesting because we are not used to thinking of teachers in language borrowed from politics. In short, the most obvious division is not always the best one.

You might choose one of the following topics to classify (unless you have in mind something that would interest you more): teachers, high school courses, children, men, women, fathers, mothers, travel experiences, care , clothing fashions, cities, sports, games, toys, movies, television programs, parties, homes, fairy tales, holidays, police, politicians, doctors

Practice 9. Sentences of Division and Classification

Division can be expressed in a variety of ways. The following are a few of the most common patterns. Notice that a number of different words can take positions A and B in the first example:

A	B
	groups
major	categories
main	classes
significant	types

a.   <u>There are</u> three <u>important kinds</u> of educational programs<u>:</u> tutorial, drill and practice, and simulation.

Notice that the words in column A all indicate that a division is informal, that it may not account for all the data. Do not use a word from column A in a sentence which introduces a formal classification, one that accounts for all the possibilities:

b.   There are three kinds of mammals: carnivores, herbivores, and omnivores.

The following passive pattern is often used to introduce both informal division and formal classification. The criterion for division is sometimes stated in an *"according to"* phrase:

c.   According to the method of instruction used, educational programs can be divided into three major groups: tutorial, drill and practice, and simulation.

The following sentence pattern introduces an informal division:

d.   Two of the important applications of the home computer are doing household chores and controlling the home environment.

You can see from these examples that one of the functions of the colon (:) is to introduce a list. The colon may introduce a "list" of divisions, or as in the following sentence, a list of examples:

e.   The computerized robot will be able to do a variety of household jobs: vacuuming, sweeping, cooking, washing dishes, taking out the garbage.

Exercise   *Write sentences of division on any of the topics introduced in this lesson. Use the preceding patterns, and make it clear by means of wording whether you are introducing an informal division or a formal classification. You might want to use some of the following divisions. The previous sentences can all be considered examples.*

1.   Computers in health care: administration, patient care.

2.   Computers in the library: record keeping, research.

3.   Computers in office communication: "electronic mail," video conferencing.

4.   Teachers: authoritarian, democratic.

5.   Modern economies: socialistic, capitalistic, mixed.

6. Electronic Funds Transfer: automatic teller machines, preauthorized banking.

7. Point of Sale Systems: keep inventory, provide daily sales report.

Practice 10. Proofreading: Modals

In Lesson 4 (Practice 11) you practiced using modals that express ability, possibility, and certainty, as in these examples:

a. Computers <u>can correct</u> certain types of writing errors.

b. We <u>may</u> (or <u>might</u> or <u>could</u>) <u>use</u> computers to teach grammar.

c. We <u>will see</u> more and more computer applications in the near future.

In these examples, notice that the modals are followed by verbs in the simple form: *correct, use, see*. Modals may be followed by more complicated verb structures (indicating progressive action or past time), but the *first* verb form after a modal is *always* in the simple form:

d. Computers <u>may be</u> changing our understanding of what a library does.

e. Fifty years ago few people <u>could have</u> imagined a robot doing household chores.

Here are some common errors in the use of modals and their corrections:

f. *Computers can <u>to</u> help diagnose illness.
    Computers can   help diagnose illness.

g. *A patient may prefer<u>s</u> to discuss problems with a computer.
    A patient may prefer to discuss problems with a computer.

h. *Computers <u>maybe</u> change the role of the teacher.
    Computers may change the role of the teacher.
(or) Maybe computers will change the role of the teacher.

Exercise   *Proofread the following paragraph, correcting any errors in the use of modals.*

COMPUTERS AND COMPOSITION

Ex: There are computer programs which are designed to help students in writing compositions. These programs can find and point out errors and to make comments on style. For example, if a student writes "the student study," the word "study" will be underlined to show there is an error. Composition programs can also finding spelling errors. Soon there maybe are programs which will automatically correct such spelling errors. Composition programs can also indicate certain kinds of punctuation errors or comment on style. For example, the computer can to inform a student of his or her average sentence length. The computer screen might shows: YOUR AVERAGE SENTENCE LENGTH IS 12 WORDS. IT MAYBE A GOOD IDEA TO WRITE SOME LONGER SENTENCES. To give another example, a composition program might pointed out that you have used the word "and" fourteen times in a paragraph of two hundred words and ask if there are any other words you could had used.

ADDITIONAL WRITING TOPICS

1. Write an essay explaining the main uses of computers in your field of study or interest. Organize by dividing those uses into general categories. If you base your essay on a reading, use paraphrase (see Lesson 5).

2. Choose an area (only one area) of important social or technological change in your country in recent years. Possible areas of change might be education, industry, social services, politics, the family, employment opportunities, village life, agriculture, or entertainment. Write an essay which divides these changes into general categories.

   Be careful that the essay you write is an essay of division. It is not enough just to write an essay on any aspect of one of these topics. Perhaps the best way to begin would be to list all the changes you can think of in one area (just as you listed all the household computer functions in the picture). Doing this will make it clear whether you have enough changes to write an essay of division. If you have enough, find a way to divide them, logically, into two or three major groups.

3. Choose a topic with which you are quite familiar (such as those in Practice 8, Exercise D) and write an essay of formal classification. Try to find a way to divide this topic that is not only logical but also informative and interesting.

Lesson Seven

COMPARING AND CONTRASTING

Subject: Personality

Contents:

—Gathering Information
—Contrast Signals
—Generalization and Support
—Organizing Comparison and Contrast
—Directed Writing: Real vs. Ideal Self
—Topic Signals
—Reviewing Thesis and Topic Sentences
—The Comparative and Superlative
—Expressing Similarity
—Word Form
—Modals
—Reviewing Signal Expressions

INTRODUCTION

In the last lesson you practiced dividing information into logical groups as a way of ordering data and organizing a composition. In this lesson, too, you will divide and organize information, but the information you will be working with is contrasting information, information that brings out the differences between two ideas, two systems, two objects, or as in this lesson, two personalities. Often the most effective way to explain something is to compare it to something else.

In Cycle One you are given drawings by two twelve-year-old children and are asked, on the basis of these drawings, to make inferences, that is, responsible or reasonable guesses, about their personalities. Using this information, you will write sentences using some of the most common contrast signals. You will also see how an essay about these two young people might be organized and developed.

In Cycle Two you will work with data from a psychological questionnaire that deals with the differences between a person's ideal self and his or her real self. The emphasis here is on finding a way to divide these differences into general groups, which will then be explained in an essay.

Adding On reviews some points from earlier lessons and introduces new organizational and grammatical material.

CYCLE ONE

Practice 1. Gathering Information

Drawings are sometimes used by psychologists and educators as indications of a child's personality, development, and perhaps, problems. Psychologists might take into consideration things which would not occur to us, the size of the drawings, for example. But many of the things that a psychologist would notice we would also notice without any special training. In these drawings, what does a smile suggest? A scream? A relaxed body? A tense one? A human form? An inhuman one? Attention to physical appearance? Indifference to appearance? A body with clear sexual identity? A body with no indication of sexual identity?

Exercise *The following personality traits might be suggested by Sally's drawing (done when she was twelve years old) and Sam's drawing (done when he was twelve years and three months old). These traits are arranged in contrasting pairs. In the blanks, write whether you think the trait describes Sally or Sam (or neither). When you finish this exercise, see if you can add to the list. Are there any other words you might use to describe Sally or Sam?*

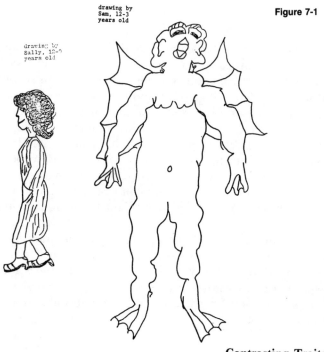

drawing by
Sam, 12-3
years old

Figure 7-1

drawing by
Sally, 12-?
years old

Contrasting Traits

Ex:	1.	_Sally_ confident	insecure	_Sam_
	2.	_____ relaxed	tense	_____
	3.	_____ immature	mature	_____
	4.	_____ realistic	imaginative	_____
	5.	_____ aware of others	less aware	_____
	6.	_____ good social skills	poor social skills	_____
	7.	_____ physically mature	physically immature	_____
	8.	_____ clear sexual identity	unformed sexual identity	_____

Can you add any words to the list?

Ex:	Sally	conformist		
Ex:	Sam	frightened		

Practice 2. Contrast Signals

A variety of words and constructions signal contrast, the most common being the word *but*. In formal writing, however, a number of other signals, both *combining* and *noncombining*, are often used. Two combining signals which indicate contrast are *while* and *whereas*. The clause containing the combining word, as usual, may take either the first (example a) or the second (examples b and c) position in the sentence:

    a.   <u>While</u> the girl in Sally's drawing appears relaxed, Sam's monster is tense.

    b.   Sam's monster is tense <u>while</u> Sally's girl appears relaxed.

    c.   Sam's monster is tense, <u>whereas</u> Sally's girl appears relaxed.

Clauses with noncombining signals are not usually set off with a comma when they are in second position (example b). Notice, however, that clauses with *whereas* (example c) usually are.

        The relationship of contrast can also be expressed by such *noncombining* signals as *however, on the other hand, in contrast, on the contrary.* Remember, a clause containing a noncombining signal is not joined to the preceding clause with a comma; it must be separated by means of a period or a semicolon. Remember, also, that noncombining expressions may take several positions in a sentence. Notice the use of commas in the following examples:

    d.   *Sally seems relaxed, <u>however,</u> Sam may be tense.

    e.   Sally seems relaxed; <u>however,</u> Sam may be tense.

    f.   Sally seems relaxed. Sam, <u>on the other hand,</u> may be tense.

Exercise   *In this exercise you are given content cues which suggest sentences of contrast about Sally and Sam. Write sentences using these cues and the signals indicated. Note: If you prefer, you may write other sentences about the drawings but try to practice using a variety of contrast signals.*

Content Cue	**Signal**
Ex: 1. mature	whereas

Whereas Sam seems childish for a twelve-year-old boy, Sally seems quite mature.

2. confident	in contrast
3. tense	whereas
4. realistic	while
5. good social skills	on the other hand
6. unformed sexual identity	however
7. aware of others	on the contrary
8. imitate others	whereas

2. _____

    _____

3. _____

    _____

4. _____

    _____

5. _____

    _____

6. _____

    _____

7. _____
   _____
8. _____
   _____

Practice 3. Generalization and Support

Sentences like "Sally seems realistic" are generalizations which would require support. Since these generalizations are interpretations of her drawing, they would have to be supported by direct reference to the drawing: What is it in the drawing itself that might give you the idea she is "realistic"?

Exercise   *Add support to the following essay, which consists entirely of generalizations. The questions in parentheses indicate how you might do this.*

SALLY AND SAM

Emotionally and socially, Sally seems more secure than Sam. She seems happier and more relaxed than he does.
1. (What is there in her drawing that indicates she is more secure, happy, relaxed?)
Ex: The girl in her drawing is smiling; Sam's monster, however, is screaming. The girl's body is relaxed, whereas the monster's body is rigid and tense. Sally also seems aware of other people and interested in them.
2. (How does the facial expression in her drawing show awareness?)

   _____
   _____.

Sam, on the other hand, shows no signs of social awareness. Indeed, the figure in his drawing is barely human at all.
3. (What nonhuman features does his monster have?)

   _____
   _____.

   In terms of sex role identification, Sally seems more mature and aware than Sam. Physically, the person in her drawing seems more like a young woman than a twelve-year-old girl.
4. (Is the girl's body mature or immature?)

   _____
   _____.

She seems very aware of clothes and physical appearance.
5. (Are her clothes and hair mature or childish?)

   _____
   _____.

The sex of Sam's monster, in contrast, is not at all clear.
6. (Is it male or female? Can you be sure?)

   _____
   _____.

It may be, however, that Sam is simply more imaginative than Sally. His drawing is certainly more interesting than hers.

7. (Why does Sam's drawing attract attention?)

_____

_____.

CYCLE TWO

Practice 4. Organizing Comparison and Contrast

An essay of contrast can be organized in two ways. For example, an essay contrasting Sally and Sam could be organized around the obvious subjects of the essay: Sally and Sam. Using this organization, you might write one paragraph all about Sally and then another all about Sam.

But the essay about Sally and Sam that you worked on in the preceding exercise was organized around more specific points, or topics: social and emotional adjustment (first paragraph) and sex role identification (second paragraph). Notice that each of these paragraphs discusses both Sally and Sam.

This type of organization is closely related to the problem you worked on in the last lesson: using general, or topic, ideas to divide and organize information. This type of organization may be a bit more difficult at first but it often results in better essays. It forces the writer to think carefully before writing and it is an easy type of organization for the reader to follow, especially in longer essays, where the general subject type of organization is usually not appropriate.

Exercise   _This exercise leads into a guided writing assignment. You will first gather information, then decide which information could be used in an essay of contrast, and finally decide how those differences might be organized—how they might be divided into groups._

The following questionnaire* concerns the differences between the way a person really is (real self) and the way he or she might prefer to be (ideal self). Rank each item on a scale of 1 (not true at all) to 4 (very true). Then mark those items which show a difference between your ideal self and your real self. Are there enough differences to serve as the basis of an essay? How can these differences be divided into paragraphs?

To the right of the questionnaire you are given sample data about "John." You might prefer to work with the data about John if you find you do not have enough differences to write about yourself, or if you would feel uncomfortable writing about your own personality.

The information about John can also serve as an example of the kind of problem you have to solve in this exercise. The first four items in the questionnaire show a dif-

*Adapted from Rick M. Gardner, _Exercises for General Psychology_ (Minneapolis, Minn.: Burgess Publishing, 1980).

ference between John's real and ideal selves. He feels he is too sensitive; he does not trust his thinking or his impulses as much as he would like; likewise, he does not trust his decisions (he keeps wondering if he is right). Do these differences have something in common? Is there a general idea that could be used to bring together these items? Could they be discussed in a single paragraph? Do the next four items (questions 5–8) have something in common? Do the last two?

Your Real Self	Your Ideal Self			John's Real Self	John's Ideal Self
———	———	1.	I am very sensitive to criticism.	3	2
———	———	2.	I trust my impulses.	2	3
———	———	3.	I trust my thinking.	2	4
———	———	4.	After making a decision, I keep wondering if I am right.	3	1
———	———	5.	I can easily express anger when I feel it.	1	2
———	———	6.	I can easily express affection when I feel it.	1	3
———	———	7.	I often behave spontaneously.	1	3
———	———	8.	Fear of embarrassment often keeps me from acting.	3	2
———	———	9.	I am often bored and apathetic.	2	2
———	———	10.	I usually have to drive myself to get things done.	2	2

Practice 5. Directed Writing: Real vs. Ideal Self

Write an essay contrasting your real and ideal selves, or if you prefer, John's real and ideal selves. Use topic idea organization.

Introduction: Write a couple of sentences of background leading to a thesis statement, which should indicate how you have divided, or organized, the information you are going to use.

Development: Write one paragraph explaining each division. Use some examples to support your ideas and make your meaning clear.

Conclusion: Restate, or summarize, your main ideas very briefly.

ADDING ON

Practice 6. Topic Signals

There is a group of expressions which can be used to make it clear to the reader that a new topic is being introduced. They are sometimes useful in writing topic sentences:

a. Concerning
Regarding   emotional adjustment, Sally seems more balanced than Sam.
With regard to
In terms of

b. As far as emotional adjustment is concerned, Sally seems more balanced than Sam.

c. Physically, the person in Sally's drawing seems more like a young woman than a girl.

The expressions in patterns a and b must be followed by noun structures, or structures which can function as nouns, such as gerunds (Lesson 4, Practice 8). They may not be followed by full clauses:

d. In terms of social awareness, Sally's girl is clearly interested in others.
   noun structure

e. In terms of being socially aware, Sally seems quite advanced.
   gerund

f. *In terms of the girl is socially aware, she is clearly interested in others.
   clause

Also, it is stylistically weak to use the same vocabulary in the main clause as in the introductory phrase:

g. *With regard to emotional adjustment, Sally seems more adjusted than Sam.

Exercise *Use the following topic cues from the real self vs. ideal self questionnaire to write sentences beginning with topic signals. You may write about yourself or about John.*

Topic Cue

1. criticism

Ex: In terms of being sensitive to criticism, John would like to be less affected by others' opinions.

2. trusting impulses

3. trusting decisions

4. expressing anger

5. expressing affection

6. behaving spontaneously

7. fear of embarrassment

8. apathy

9. motivation

Practice 7. Reviewing Thesis and Topic Sentences

As you learned in the last lesson, the thesis statement indicates the overall point, or purpose, of an essay. The thesis statement is usually in the first, or introductory, paragraph. Similarly, the topic sentence indicates the main point, or purpose, of a single paragraph. The following essay concerns the different personality traits of a "typical" firstborn and a "typical" last born child. There is no thesis statement in the introduction; there are no topic sentences in the other two paragraphs. How is the information in the second paragraph different from the information in the third paragraph? Can you write topic sentences that cover the information in each paragraph? Then can you go back to the beginning and add a thesis statement?

FIRSTBORNS VS. LAST BORNS

1   A great many things influence the formation of our personalities: our culture, our parents, our experiences, and perhaps even our biological makeup. Psychologists who have studied the family have found that one of the factors influencing personality is birth order. This can be seen very
5   clearly by contrasting the personalities of the typical firstborn and the typical last born. (Thesis) _____

_____
_____.

(Topic) _____

10   _____
_____. The firstborn often has a stronger sense of responsibility and independence than the last born. Psychologists have also noticed that the firstborn often pushes himself or herself harder than the last born. This desire to succeed may be a result of the dissatisfac-

15 tion with themselves that many firstborns seem to feel. Psychologists think this dissatisfaction may date from the birth of the second child, when the firstborn loses his or her favored position in the family.
(Topic)

_____

_____

20 _____

In dealing with others, firstborns tend to be aggressive, to be leaders, to control the situation. Last borns, on the other hand, are more relaxed in social groups and are often better companions. Last borns are also more sensitive to the feelings of others, reacting to emotions and needs that a
25 firstborn might not even notice. It is not difficult to understand the last born's ease with others: The last born has always been surrounded by others and enjoyed their attention. He or she has never had to feel displaced or jealous like the firstborn.

Practice 8. The Comparative and the Superlative

The contrast signals studied in Practice 2 of this lesson are not the only means of expressing contrast or difference. A group of patterns like the following are traditionally called the *comparative:*

   a. Sam is more imaginative than Sally.

A similar group of patterns, used to compare more than two of something, is called the *superlative:*

   b. Of all the children in the group, Sam is the most imaginative.

What follows is a brief summary of comparative and superlative patterns. Notice that the patterns differ somewhat according to whether the key word is an adjective or a noun and that it sometimes makes a difference whether the noun is count or noncount.

Adjectives

Comparative	**Superlative**
a. Andrew is calmer than Mickey.	Andrew is the calmest in his family.
b. Stefan is more secure than Sean.	He is the most secure in his class.
c. Matthew is less talkative than Jenny.	She is the least shy in her family.

Nouns

Comparative	**Superlative**
d. Sam's drawing shows more imagination than Sally's.	Matthew shows the most talent in drawing.
e. John has less self-control than Mark. (*Noncount noun.*)	Michael has the least self-control of the three.
f. Paul has fewer worries than Jim. (*Count noun.*)	Fred has the fewest worries of anyone I know.

Exercise   *Write sentences about the following people using the comparative or the superlative (4 = very true; 1 = not true at all). Note: Use <u>has</u> not <u>is</u> before nouns (see examples e and f).*

	John	Mary	James
Ex:			
1. sensitive to criticism	3	2	4
<u>James is the most sensitive to criticism.</u>			
(or) <u>Mary is less sensitive to criticism than John or James.</u>			
2. aware of others	3	2	3
3. critical of others	2	3	1
4. problems	2	3	4
5. kind	3	2	4
6. affectionate	3	2	2
7. spontaneous	2	4	1

Practice 9. Expressing Similarity

At times, of course, you will want to point out the similarity between two things rather than the differences. A number of patterns can be used to do this. The *as . . . as* pattern can be used with adjectives and nouns. Notice the use of *much* with noncount nouns and *many* with count nouns.

a.   Bill is <u>as</u> spontaneous <u>as</u> John. (*Spontaneous* is an adjective.)

b.   Betty has <u>as much</u> social awareness <u>as</u> Sally. (*Awareness* is a noncount noun.)

c.   Betty has <u>as many</u> friends <u>as</u> Sally. (*Friends* is a count noun.)

The word *like* can also express similarity. It must be followed by a noun structure or one which can function as a noun, such as a gerund (example e). Notice also that the *like* phrase can take different positions in the sentence and is punctuated with commas:

    d. <u>Like</u> Sam, Bill has an active imagination.

    e. Having confidence in one's decisions, <u>like</u> trusting one's emotions, is a sign of security.

Clearly all the patterns of similarity just discussed express contrast when made negative:

    f. David <u>does not</u> have <u>as many</u> worries <u>as</u> James.

    g. Bill, <u>un</u>like Sam, is a very social child.

A group of noncombining signals (*in the same way, likewise, similarly*) also indicate similarity:

    h. Susan often keeps wondering if she has made the right decision; <u>in the same way</u> (or <u>likewise</u> or <u>similarly</u>), Virginia questions her judgment.

In this example, both halves of the sentence express the same idea but in different words: "questions her judgment" paraphrases "keeps wondering if she has made the right decision." It is better style to use paraphrase than direct repetition:

    i. *Susan often keeps wondering if she has made the right decision; likewise, Virginia often keeps wondering if she has made the right decision.

Exercise *Rewrite the following sentences using the pattern suggested by the word(s) given in parentheses. The first sentence, for example, expresses similarity using* like; *it is rewritten with the* as . . . as *pattern, as suggested in parentheses. Note: It may be necessary to make several changes to produce a grammatical sentence.*

Ex: 1. Like John, I am sensitive to criticism. (as . . . as)
       <u>I am as sensitive to criticism as John.</u>

    2. Katherine often behaves spontaneously. Mark often acts without reflecting. (in the same way)

    3. Like Andrew, Matthew has difficulty expressing anger. (as . . . as)

    4. Jan expresses emotions easily. June is open with her feelings. (likewise)

5. Jim and Edward both leave a lot of things unfinished. (as . . . as)

6. Firstborns are often very responsible. They are often rather independent. (similarly)

7. Firstborns are often ambitious. Younger children are sometimes quite ambitious. (like)

Practice 10. Word Form

As you know, many English words vary their word form according to their grammatical function, as in these examples:

a. Firstborns <u>tend</u> to be <u>ambitious</u> and <u>aggressive.</u>
         verb   adjective   adjective

b. Last borns have a <u>tendency</u> to pursue their <u>ambitions</u>
                 noun   noun
   less <u>aggressively.</u>
      adverb

This is worth keeping in mind because the following type of error is very common:

c. *John is very <u>ambition.</u>

d. *Everyone wants to <u>success.</u>

It is important to be aware of word form not only to avoid basic errors like those just given but also to use correctly certain more advanced structures. To give just one example, in this lesson you have seen that topic signals like *regarding* in the following must be followed by a noun structure:

e. Regarding <u>self-confidence,</u> I would like to be a bit surer of myself.

Questions of form and grammatical function are not limited to single words. You have seen, for example, (Lesson 4, Practice 8) that entire clauses can be changed in form so that they can function as nouns. A clause like that in example *f* might be changed to a complex noun phrase as in example *g*, or a gerund phrase as in example *h*:

   f. Last borns consider the feelings of others.

   g. <u>Last borns' consideration of the feelings of others</u> makes them easy to get along with.

   h. Last borns differ from firstborns in social sensitivity, for example, in <u>their considering the feelings of others</u>.

Exercise *Fill in the blanks in the second of each pair of sentences with the correct form of the word or words that are italicized in the first sentence. You can check your answers in a dictionary, where you will usually find the following abbreviations used:* n. (*noun*), v.t. *or* v.i. (*verb, transitive or intransitive*), adj. (*adjective*), adv. (*adverb*).

Ex: 1. Sam may not be as *confident* as Sally.
                (adjective)
           Sam may not have as much __confidence__ as Sally.
                                (noun)

  2. Sally seems *socially adjusted*.
      This _____ _____ can be seen in the facial expression of the girl in her drawing.

  3. Sally's drawing indicates she is *socially secure*.
      Sally's drawing indicates _____ in _____ situations.

  4. *Sam may be insecure.*
      _____ could result in poor relations with other children.

  5. Sam is an *imaginative* boy.
      Sam may not be insecure; he may just have a good _____.

  6. *The girl is smiling.*
      _____ shows that she is aware of the impression she makes on others.

  7. Sam may express his feelings *spontaneously*.
      The violent emotion of the monster suggests _____.

  8. Sally's *reaction* to praise is very *positive*.
      She probably _____ _____ to praise.

  9. *Sam fantasizes.*
      _____ may indicate either a healthy imagination or a desire to escape from reality.

10. Mary is very *critical* of others' *behavior*.
      She _____ the way people _____.

11. *James controls his emotions carefully.*
      _____ makes him seem cold to some people.

12. John is *kind* and *affectionate*.
      He shows his _____ and _____ in many ways.

13. Firstborn children may feel their parents are *rejecting* them when a second child is *born*.
      The _____ of a second child may create feelings of _____ in the firstborn child.

Practice 11. Modals

In Lesson 4 (Practice 11) you saw that a group of words called *modals* could be used to indicate the degree of certainty you felt about a future situation. Modals can again be used to express the degree of certainty you feel about the inferences you have been making:

Certain

Possible

a. Sally <u>must</u> <u>be</u> a very social girl.
b. Sam <u>may</u> <u>express</u> his feelings spontaneously.
c. He <u>might</u> <u>have</u> feelings of anger.
d. At times he <u>could</u> <u>become</u> violently angry.

Notice, first, that *must* here is being used to express certainty, not obligation. *Must* in example *a* is completely different from *must* in this sentence: Papers *must* be turned in by next Friday. Secondly, *must* is much stronger than *may*, but *may* is only slightly stronger than *might*, and *might* only somewhat stronger than *could*.

Out of context it is impossible to say whether a sentence like "He may work" refers to the habitual present or the future: there is no difference in form: modal + simple form of the verb. It is possible, however, to indicate past time when there is a modal:

e. He <u>may have worked</u> yesterday. (Modal + HAVE + Past Participle)

It is also possible to indicate that the meaning is progressive, either present/future or past:

f. He <u>may be</u> working right now/tomorrow (Modal + BE + Verb-ING)

g. He <u>may have been</u> working last night when I called.
(Modal + HAVE + BEEN + Verb-ING)

These possibilities may be summarized as follows:

	Present/Future	*Past*
Simple	He may work.	He may have worked.
Progressive	He may be working.	He may have been working.

Any of these sentences can be made negative by adding *not* right after the modal:

h. Sam may <u>not</u> be an angry child.

Notice, however, that in the negative the meaning of *could* changes in sentences such as these. In the negative it expresses certainty like *must:*

i. Sally <u>could not</u> have been shy. = Sally <u>must not</u> have been shy.

Exercise   *The sentences that follow are statements about Sally and Sam. By adding modals, express your opinion as to whether the ideas are possibly or almost certainly true. You may want to make some of the sentences negative. Pay attention to whether the sentences express progressive meaning and whether they have a past or present focus.*

Ex: 1.   Sam is a nervous child.
<u>Sam may be a nervous child.</u> (or) <u>Sam must be a nervous child.</u>

Ex: 2.   Sally was a neat girl.
<u>Sally must have been a neat girl.</u>

3.   Sam's monster is expressing anger.

4.   Sam used monster fantasies to escape from his worries.

5.   Sally pays a lot of attention to physical appearance.

6.   The girl in Sally's drawing is older than Sally herself.

7.   Sally was fantasizing that she was older than twelve.

8.   Sam was frustrated about something when he drew the monster.

9.   Sam has conflicting emotions.

10.   Something is bothering Sam.

11.   Sam was expressing hostility when he drew his picture.

Practice 12. Reviewing Signal Expressions

In this book you have been introduced to a variety of signal expressions: time signals, example signals, restatement signals, list signals, step signals, contrast signals, and topic signals. As your writing becomes more advanced, you will become aware that a single paragraph or a single essay will often involve a variety of logical relations, and perhaps a variety of signal expressions to make those relations clear. In an earlier lesson, such as Lesson 2, a paragraph might have very simply consisted of a generalization and a couple of examples. A paragraph might, however, be developed in more complex ways. It might, for example, state a generalization, restate it, give an example of it, contrast one idea with another, add another point, give an example, and so on. The short essay in the following exercise, for example, makes use of generalization, restatement, examples, contrast, and addition ("listing").

Exercise.   *Fill in the blanks in the following essay using the signal expressions in the following list. Use each one once. There is some freedom in the order in which you may choose to use them:*

moreover	in other words	also
for example	for instance	as regards
in terms of	whereas	however

MY REAL AND IDEAL SELVES

    Comparing my real self and my ideal self, I find two things I would like to change. I would like to be more sure of myself and more able to express my emotions openly.

Ex: <u>In terms of</u> self confidence, there are several indications that I am a bit insecure. _____, I am very sensitive to criticism. If I get a low grade on a composition, _____, I get upset, _____ I should just accept my mistakes and try to learn from them. I am _____ too easily pleased by praise, probably because it increases my confidence in myself. _____, I often do not trust my own thinking and judgment as much as I should. After I reach a decision, I sometimes keep wondering if it is the right one.

    _____ emotional expression, I would like to be able to express my feelings openly and easily. _____, I find it difficult to express both affection and anger. I would like, _____, to be less reserved, to be more spontaneous.

ADDITIONAL WRITING TOPICS

1. Compare and contrast the personalities of two people you know.
2. Research one of the following topics in psychology and write an essay of comparison or contrast: type A vs. type B personality, birth order and personality, the psychology of sex differences.
3. Compare and contrast two generations in your country.
4. Compare and contrast one family role in two different cultures, for example, the American father vs. the father in your culture or the American mother vs. the mother in your culture. Limit yourself to one role but deal with it in some detail; in other words, do not contrast the entire American family with the family in your country.
5. Compare and contrast a social institution in the United States and in your country. Possible topics might be such things as education, health care, the police, the military, and so on. Or you might prefer to discuss only your country, contrasting an institution such as education now and, say, fifty years ago.
6. Contrast the American way of doing business and the way of doing business in your country.

7. The masculine and feminine traits that follow are taken from a psychology questionnaire used to measure "masculinity" and "femininity."* Write an essay contrasting the ideas of masculinity and femininity as they are defined by this questionnaire. Or since these definitions are questionable, you might prefer to contrast your definition of masculinity or femininity (not both) with the definition implied in the questionnaire. For example, the questionnaire says that being "childlike" is a feminine trait. Do you agree?

Masculine Traits	**Feminine Traits**
self-reliant	yielding
independent	tender
individualistic	loyal
defends own beliefs	affectionate
strong personality	understanding
competitive	shy
ambitious	childlike
aggressive	loves children
dominant	likes flattery
analytic	gullible
	cheerful

*Adapted from Rick M. Gardner, *Exercises for General Psychology* (Minneapolis, Minn.: Burgess Publishing, 1980).

Lesson Eight

USING AND INTERPRETING STATISTICS

Subject: The Changing American Family

Contents:

INTRODUCTION

In this lesson, which deals with recent changes in the American family, you will again practice making and supporting generalizations. In this lesson, however, you will practice using statistics, rather than specific examples, as support.

After studying these statistics, you will also try to interpret them, that is, offer possible explanations for the changes that have occurred. You will, in other words, be introduced to the notions of cause and result, ideas that will be further developed in the following two lessons.

Cycle One introduces a variety of statistics from the 1980 U.S. Census. The discussion questions are designed to make sure you understand the statistics and to help you start thinking about their significance.

Cycle Two provides more specific practice in writing generalization, support, and interpretation. It concludes with an essay on the changing American family.

Adding On provides further exercises on the kind of grammar and organization involved in writing academic essays.

CYCLE ONE

Practice 1. Reading

*SAN FRANCISCO: A CITY OF SINGLES**

1   The advertisements for an expensive apartment development in South San Francisco are aimed at a new kind of buyer here. "You don't have to be married to buy a home," the ads announce.

Indeed, about one-third of the people who are buying the devel-
5   opment's apartments are not married. They are among the nation's continually increasing number of what the U.S. Bureau of the Census calls "nonfamily households," that is, households consisting of a person living alone or with nonrelatives.

And they have made San Francisco the country's first "city of
10   singles." The 1980 census found that of all households in this city of 679,000, the majority—53 percent—were of the nonfamily type. In 1970 the rate was 44 percent.

Population analysts attribute the sharp growth of singles to several trends, including the greatly increased number of divorces and
15   separations, the postponement or rejection of marriage by young adults, and the rising number of older people living by themselves after the death of a husband or wife.

*Adapted from Philip Hager, "New Majority—the Singles," *Los Angeles Times*, Oct. 26, 1982. Copyright, 1982, Los Angeles Times. Reprinted by permission.

Questions

1. What is the definition of a "nonfamily household" in this article?
2. Are married couples counted as family or nonfamily households? A brother and a sister living together? College roommates? A boyfriend and girlfriend? A divorced mother and her child?
3. How did living arrangements in San Francisco change between 1970 and 1980?
4. What statistics support this generalization?
5. How do experts explain or interpret this trend? What are the three reasons given in the article?
6. Why do you think some young people postpone marriage? What might be the advantages to marrying late?
7. Why do you think more people are rejecting marriage altogether?
8. The article says more people are living alone after the death of their husband or wife. Who did they use to live with after the death of their spouse?
9. Do you have any idea why the divorce rate is rising? Do you feel certain about this interpretation or do you feel you are making a guess?

Practice 2. Formal Definition

You have already practiced defining terms which may be unclear to your reader (Lesson 3, Practices 2 and 8). Before continuing to study the statistics in this lesson, it is important to be sure you understand the terms used by the U.S. Bureau of the Census. At the same time you can review the patterns of definition you already know and learn some patterns used in formal definition.

As you saw in Lesson 3, nonrestrictive adjective clauses and appositives can be used to define a term. The definition may be introduced by the signal expression *that is*:

a. More people live in nonfamily households, <u>(which are)</u> households consisting of a person living alone or with nonrelatives.

b. More people live in nonfamily households, <u>that is</u>, households consisting of a person living alone or with nonrelatives.

Several other rather formal patterns may be used to define a term. Notice that the source of the definition may be given in an *according to* phrase:

c. The U.S. Bureau of the Census <u>defines</u> a nonfamily household <u>as</u> a person living alone or with nonrelatives.

d. <u>According to</u> the U.S. Bureau of the Census, a nonfamily household <u>is defined as</u> a person living alone or with nonrelatives.

e. A nonfamily household <u>refers to</u> (or <u>means</u>) a person living alone or with nonrelatives.

f. According to the U.S. Bureau of the Census, a <u>nonfamily household is a household which</u> consists of a person living alone or with nonrelatives.

Notice that this last pattern can only be used to define something that is a specific instance of a general idea: *Household* is a general idea; *nonfamily household* is a more specific instance, or subtype. In the following exercise only the terms *one-parent family* and *unmarried couple* could be defined by using this pattern.

Exercise   *Using the preceding patterns (especially the ones that are new to this lesson), write sentences defining the following terms used by the U.S. Bureau of the Census.*

	Term	**Definition**
1.	household	all the persons who occupy a housing unit
2.	family	a group of persons related by birth, marriage, or adoption and living together
3.	one-parent family	a family headed by just the mother or just the father
4.	unmarried couple	two unrelated adults of opposite sex sharing a housing unit
5.	marriage rate	the number of marriages per year for every 1,000 unmarried women aged 15 to 44
6.	divorce ratio	the number of currently divorced people per every 1,000 currently married people

a. _____

_____

b. _____

_____

c. _____

_____

d. _____

_____

e. _____

_____

f. _____

_____

Practice 3. Understanding and Interpreting Statistics

In the following pages a variety of statistics on the changing American family are presented. These statistics will later be used to support generalizations, which you will then try to interpret.

The questions which follow the table and the two graphs are divided into two groups, the first group focusing on the meaning of the statistics, the second on possible ways to interpret them.

Table 8-1   Marriage, Fertility and Divorce for Selected Years

	1967	1970	1980	1983
Marriage rate		140.2	102.6	
Median age at marriage, men		23.2 yrs.		25.4 yrs.
Median age, women		20.8 yrs.		22.8 yrs.
Children *expected* by married women, 18–34	3.1			2.2
Unmarried couple households		523,000		1,891,000
Divorce ratio		47		114

Sources: U.S. Bureau of the Census, *Current Population Reports.* Series P-20, Nos 389,391 and U.S. National Center for Health Statistics, *Vital Statistics of the United States, 1984.*

Table 8-1

In considering the data in Table 8-1 be sure you understand what the terms mean. The marriage rate here refers to the number of marriages per year for every 1,000 unmarried women between 15 and 44. The exact meaning of *median age* is more complicated than you need to know here; for now it is enough to understand that a rise in the median age at marriage corresponds to a rise in the average age at marriage. The divorce ratio gives the number of divorced people for every 1,000 married persons. Note: These statistics are *not* percentages; be sure you understand the unit of measurement.

Questions: Understanding

1. How much did the marriage rate decrease between 1970 and 1980?
2. If an American city had exactly 2,000 unmarried women between the ages of 15 and 44, how many of them would have gotten married in 1970? In 1980?
3. Did the median age at marriage increase or decrease between 1970 and 1983?
4. In 1967 the number of children the average American woman expected to have was (a) 3, (b) 4, (c) 5.
5. Are Americans having more or fewer children?
6. How many unmarried households were there in 1983?
7. The divorce ratio increased from 47 in 1970 to 114 in 1983. That is an increase of more than (a) 50%, (b) 100%, (c) 200%

Questions: Interpretation

8. Why do you think Americans are marrying later?
9. Why do you think the marriage rate is decreasing?
10. Why do you think Americans are having fewer children?
11. Why do you think more couples are choosing to live together without getting married?
12. Do you have any opinion about the causes of divorce in the U.S.?

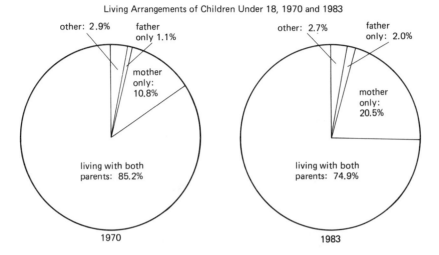

Figure 8-1   Living Arrangements of Children Under 18, 1970 and 1983

Source: U.S. Bureau of the Census, *Current Population Reports*, Series P-20, no. 389.

Figure 8-1

Figure 8-1 provides statistics about the living arrangements of children, in other words, who they lived with, in 1970 and in 1983. All the statistics are percentages.

Questions: Understanding
1. How much did the percentage of children living with both their mother and father decrease between 1970 and 1983?
2. In 1983, out of every 100 children, how many were *not* living with both their parents?
3. In 1970 10.8% lived with their mother only whereas in 1983 20.5% did. That is an increase of almost (a) 10%, (b) 50%, (c) 100%.
4. What does it mean to say that in 1983 2.7% were living with "other"? Can you give any examples?

Questions: Interpretation
5. What do you think is the main reason for this increase in the number of children living with one parent?
6. Can you think of any other possible explanations for this increase?

Figure 8-2

Figure 8-2 presents data on the percentages of women working in civilian (non-military) jobs in 1950, 1970, and 1982. All these statistics are in percentages.

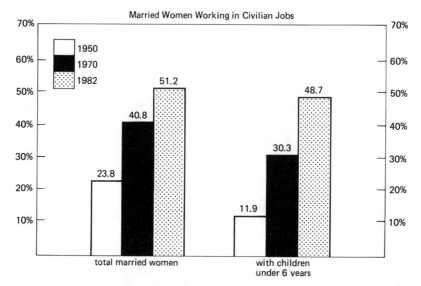

Figure 8-2 Married Women Working in Civilian Jobs

Source: U.S. Bureau of the Census, *Current Population Reports,* Series P-20, no. 373 and P-23, no. 130.

Questions: Understanding

1. How much did the percentage of all married women working increase between 1950 and 1982?
2. What percentage of women with children under the age of six worked in 1950? In 1970? In 1982?
3. The group which shows the greatest percentage of increase between 1950 and 1982 is (a) all married women, (b) married women with children under the age of six.

Questions: Interpretation

4. Why do you think more women are working?
5. Do you think some women who do not have to work choose to work? Why?
6. Where do most children under the age of six stay while their mothers work?

CYCLE TWO

Practice 4. Using Statistics for Support

Statistics are an extremely effective way to support a generalization. This kind of generalization and support may be combined in a single sentence or expressed in more than one sentence, as in the example that follows. Notice that the source of the information is stated in the sentence of generalization:

a. <u>Source:</u>   It is clear from U.S. Bureau of the Census statistics that the
    <u>Generalization:</u>   number of divorced people in the population increased dramat-
    <u>Support:</u>   ically between 1970 and 1983. In 1970 there were 47 divorced
                               people for every 1,000 married people while in 1983 there were
                               114.

There are a number of ways to include a source in a sentence. The following
patterns are three of the most common:

b. <u>According to the U.S. Bureau of the Census</u>, the number of divorced people in the
    population has increased dramatically.

c. U.S. Bureau of the Census statistics <u>show</u> (or <u>indicate</u> or <u>make it clear</u>) <u>that</u> the
    number of divorced people in the population has increased dramatically.

d. <u>It can be seen from</u> (or <u>It is clear from, It is evident from</u>) U.S. Bureau of the Census
    statistics <u>that</u> the number of divorced people in the population has increased
    dramatically.

Exercise *The following questions can be answered by using the information presented in the
preceding table and graphs. Answer each question with a generalization and then
support that generalization with a statistic. This will often require two sentences. Use
the sentence patterns just given to include the source of your information, which is the
U.S. Bureau of the Census.*

Ex: 1. Were fewer children living with both parents in 1970 or 1983?
             <u>U.S. Bureau of the Census statistics make it clear that fewer children lived
             with both parents in 1983 than in 1970. The number decreased from 85.2%
             to 74.9%.</u>

         2. Did the marriage rate decrease between 1970 and 1980?

         3. Were people marrying later in 1983 than in 1970?

         4. Did women in 1983 plan to have fewer children than in 1967?

         5. Were more people living together without being married in 1970 or 1983?

6. Has the number of working women with young children been increasing?

Practice 5. Cause/Result Signals

An essay dealing with the changing American family would not stop with generalizations and statistical support. It would also try to interpret or explain the changes discussed; it would, in other words, deal with causes and their results, for example:

Cause: people marrying later

Result: increase in nonfamily households

There are a number of signal expressions which make this relationship clear. There are, first, two *combining cause signals, because* and *since.* They introduce the clause stating a cause:

a. The number of nonfamily households is increasing, in part, *because* (or *since*) people are marrying later.

There is also a group of *noncombining result signals: therefore, consequently, for this reason, as a result.* These signals are placed in the result clause:

b. Many people are choosing to marry later. For this reason (or therefore, consequently, as a result), the number of nonfamily households is increasing.

Signals of this type, you will remember, do not join clauses; they may also take a number of positions in the result clause:

c. The number of nonfamily households is, therefore, increasing.

Another type of *cause signal* must be followed by a noun structure or one that can function as a noun, such as a gerund (see Lesson 4, Practice 8). Three such signals are *because of, due to,* and *as a result of.* (Notice that *as a result,* mentioned previously, is a result signal, whereas *as a result of* is a cause signal.)

d. As a result of (or because of or due to) divorce, the number of family households is decreasing.

e. In part, the decrease in the number of family households is due to people postponing marriage. (Gerund phrase functioning as noun/object.)

The following sentence pattern is one more way to signal *cause/result:*

f. One of the reasons for (or causes of) the decrease in the number of family households is divorce.

In this pattern notice that the result (decrease) follows the signal expression, whereas the cause (divorce) follows the verb *be*. In this pattern both the result and the cause must be stated in noun structures or structures which can function as nouns.

Exercise *Write sentences of cause/result interpreting the following generalizations. The generalizations you are given may express a cause, a result, or either. The first generalization, for example (people are getting married later), could be considered either a result of career pressure, among other things, or one of the causes of the decrease in the number of children in the average family. As an example it is done both ways. You may not want to use the exact words given; you may prefer to paraphrase the idea, as in the first of these examples:*

Ex: 1. People are getting married later.
<u>People need time to finish their educations or begin a career; as a result, they are postponing marriage.</u> (Postponing marriage = result of education and careers.)

(or) <u>Because people are marrying later, the size of the average family is decreasing.</u> (Marrying later = cause of decreasing family size.)

2. The number of one-parent households has increased.

3. The marriage rate is decreasing.

4. Americans are having fewer children.

5. The number of unmarried couples has increased.

6. Divorces have become much more common.

7. More women are working.

8. More preschool children go to day-care centers.

Practice 6. Directed Writing: The Changing American Family

Write a short essay on *one* of the following topics, using statistics from this lesson:

Changes in Marriage Patterns
Changes in Childraising
Changes in the Role of Women

The best way to get started might be to go through the tables and graphs again, finding the statistics that relate to the topic you have chosen. Then choose the ones you want to use. Do not get lost in the statistics. It is not necessary to use every statistic that relates to your topic; select a few that will clearly support your generalizations.

When you are ready to begin writing you may want to organize your essay like this:

First Paragraph: Describe the changes that have taken place, supporting your generalizations with statistics.

Second Paragraph: Interpret those changes. Remember, there may be several factors responsible for a single change; you might find you want more than one paragraph to discuss them.

ADDING ON

Practice 7. Repeating for Clarity: Paraphrase

Academic writing often uses a good deal of repetition to make complex ideas clear. As you have seen (Lesson 3, Practice 7), certain pronouns can be used to avoid too much direct repetition:

a.   The marriage rate fell between 1970 and 1980. One of the reasons for <u>this</u> is that people are getting married later.

The pronoun *this* could be considered a kind of paraphrase of the words *the marriage rate fell between 1970 and 1980.* Other types of paraphrase may be used to repeat an idea for clarity. The original wording may be repeated with a change in word form (example b), partially paraphrased (example c), or completely paraphrased (example d):

b.   The <u>marriage rate fell</u> between 1970 and 1980. The <u>falling marriage rate</u> is due partly to the postponement of marriage.

c.   The <u>marriage rate fell</u> between 1970 and 1980. The <u>declining marriage rate</u> is due partly to the postponement of marriage.

d. The <u>marriage rate fell</u> between 1970 and 1980. <u>This decline</u> is due partly to the postponement of marriage.

Exercise   *The following essay contains too much direct repetition, which is italicized. Improve the style of the essay by changing the direct repetition to the kinds of indirect repetition just studied. There is, of course, no one correct answer to this exercise: It can be done in several ways. Remember also that **some** direct repetition is not necessarily bad.*

THE INCREASE IN NONFAMILY HOUSEHOLDS

Ex: A great many factors are responsible for the dramatic increase in the
1.   number of nonfamily households. One of the *factors responsible for the*
Ex: <u>reasons that many more people are living with nonrelatives</u>
dramatic increase in the number of nonfamily households is that people
2.   tend to get married later now than they used to. Some young people *get married later now* so that they can enjoy a longer period free from responsibil-
3.   ity. This *period free from responsibility* gives them more time to decide on a career, study, travel, or pursue their personal interests.
4.   Women especially may choose *to get married later now than they used to.* They may want to establish themselves in a career before taking on the responsi-
5.   bility of raising a family. These women may feel that if they do not *establish themselves in a career before raising a family,* they may have a hard time ever
6.   *establishing themselves in a career.* Indeed, for this reason some women decide not to marry at all.
7.   Other changes in living patterns also contribute to *the increase in the number of nonfamily households.* One of these changes is the increase in divorce. After a divorce, a man or woman living without children would be counted as a
8.   nonfamily household. Another change in *living patterns which contributes to the increase in nonfamily households* is the greater tendency of people to live to-
9.   gether without getting married. *People who live together without getting married* are considered nonfamily households.

Practice 8. The Conclusion

The directed writing exercises in this book have often suggested ways to conclude your essays. But the question of how to write a conclusion has not been dealt with in detail yet.

In general, the concluding paragraph of an essay makes use of one or more of the following devices: restatement, further generalization, evaluation. These three points will be discussed after you have considered an example. The following paraphrase of the introductory reading, "San Francisco: A City of Singles," includes a paragraph of conclusion.

1   The 1980 U.S. Census revealed that San Francisco has become a city of singles. In 1980 fewer San Franciscans were living in family households than in nonfamily households, which the Census Bureau defines as households consisting of a person living alone or with non-

5

relatives. In other words, fewer people were living with people to whom they were related by either blood or marriage; they were, instead, living alone or with friends, boyfriends, girlfriends, or simply, roommates.

10

In 1980 53 percent of all the households in San Francisco (a city of 679,000) were nonfamily households. This reflects a significant change from 1970, when nonfamily households accounted for only 44 percent of the total number of households in the city. The percentage of nonfamily households increased by 9 percent in ten years.

15

20

Population analysts think this change has several causes. First, the number of divorces and separations also increased between 1970 and 1980. A divorced person living without children is counted as a nonfamily household. Second, many young adults are deciding to postpone marriage or not to get married at all. Another reason has to do with older people who have lost their spouse. In 1980 more of these people were living alone than in 1970, when more were, presumably, living with a relative, most often a son or daughter.

Restatement:

Further Generalization:

Evaluation:

In brief, then, changes in marriage patterns and family structure have significantly changed living arrangements in San Francisco. These changes may have come about more quickly in San Francisco than in other cities, but the same trends are found in many major American cities. They are trends that, to some, indicate a healthy diversity or freedom of choice and, to others, a dangerous weakening of the family.

The first thing to notice about a conclusion is that it should be short. If it is not you are probably introducing material that should have been dealt with earlier in the essay.

Of the three devices mentioned—restatement, further generalization, and evaluation—restatement is the most important in an academic essay: You will most often close an essay by restating your general idea, whether or not you choose to add further generalization and evaluation. There are two things to notice about a concluding restatement. First, only the main ideas of the essay are restated, and they are restated in extremely general terms. The first two paragraphs of the essay are summarized in the first sentence of the conclusion. None of the supporting or developing material from the essay is repeated in the conclusion; statistics and definitions, for example, are not restated. The second thing to notice about a concluding restatement is that if possible it *paraphrases* the main ideas; it does not repeat them directly. The phrases "marriage patterns," "family structure," and "living arrangements," for example, were not used until the conclusion.

Whereas most conclusions involve restatement, further generalization is sometimes useful, other times not. In the essay dealing with San Francisco it is quite natural, at the end, to consider whether the trends in this city are similar to or different from those in other cities: The trends can be further generalized to other cities. It might also be possible to further generalize in time, to say, for example, that the trends discussed may very well continue into the future. To give another example, you might want to consider whether the trends you wrote about in the directed essay in this lesson can be further generalized to other countries. Do not, however, use further generalization unless it makes sense to do so. It is a possible but not a necessary element in a concluding paragraph.

The concluding paragraph of an academic essay sometimes includes evaluation, or judgment. You may evaluate the reliability of the data used or express how certain you feel about the ideas raised. Or if you wish to give a personal reaction or opinion, it should be placed in the concluding paragraph. Be careful, though: A personal opinion is not always appropriate in an academic essay. Notice that the "opinion" expressed at the end of the sample concluding paragraph is not really a personal one: Two possible contradictory opinions are both briefly stated. You will have to use your judgment in deciding how much personal opinion would be appropriate in a particular paper.

Finally, you may have noticed that the concluding paragraph began with the words *in brief.* This expression and the others that follow are *noncombining conclusion signals.* They are often placed at or near the beginning of a concluding paragraph: *in brief, briefly, in summary, to summarize, in conclusion, to conclude, in short, in a word.*

Exercise   *Go back to the directed essay you wrote in Practice 6 of this lesson (or if you prefer, the essay in Practice 7) and add a concluding paragraph. Be sure to use restatement in your paragraph; decide whether to use further generalization and evaluation.*

Practice 9. Emphatic Restatement Signals

You have seen that the expressions *that is* and *in other words* can be used to define or explain a preceding term or idea, to restate it in different words (Lesson 3, Practice 8):

   a.   More families are being run by an "unmarried head," <u>that is</u> (or <u>in other words</u>), an adult who is single, separated, divorced, or widowed.

In the following examples, the second sentence restates the idea in the first sentence, but in stronger terms. This might be called *emphatic restatement* and be signaled by *indeed* or *in fact:*

   b.   Many children like day care<u>.</u> <u>Indeed</u>, they may like it better than staying home.

   c.   More couples were living together without being married in 1983 than in 1970. The number of unmarried households more than tripled<u>,</u> <u>in fact.</u>

Indeed and *in fact* are noncombining signals and may take different positions in a sentence. Notice again how such signals are punctuated. Notice also that in emphatic restatement the idea is sometimes repeated in more specific terms (*more than tripled* in example c).

Exercise   *In the following sentences decide whether the restatement is emphatic or not. If it is, fill in the blank with **indeed** or **in fact**; if it is not, fill in the blank with **that is** or **in other words.***

Ex: 1.   More people are living with nonrelatives, __that is__, with people they are not related to by birth or marriage.

Ex: 2.   The marriage rate (for unmarried women, 15–44) was lower in 1980 than in 1970. __Indeed__, it dropped from 140 per 1,000 to 103 per 1,000.

3.   There has been a sharp increase in the number of one-parent households. _____, more children are being raised by one parent.

4.   Family size has been decreasing; _____, people are having fewer children.

5.   There were more divorced people in the population in 1983 than in 1970. _____, the number more than doubled.

6.   Children are expensive; _____, it costs a lot to raise a child in a modern society. _____, the total cost of raising a child and putting him or her through college is over $100,000 for the average family.

7.   Many young people prefer to live together as "unmarried couples," _____, without getting married.

8.   There were a great many unmarried couple households in 1983. There were, _____, nearly two million such households in the population.

9.   The number of married women working has been steadily increasing in recent years. _____, in 1982 more than 50 percent of all married women worked.

10.   Almost half the women with preschool children, _____, children under the age of six, worked in 1982.

Practice 10. Possibility, Probability, and Certainty

In this lesson, as in the last one, you have been interpreting or making inferences. You may, or may not, be certain about the conclusions you draw. To give an example, you may or may not feel certain that day care is good for preschoolers.

As you saw in the last lesson (in Practice 11) modals are often used to express possibility, probability, or certainty:

a.   Children's social skills <u>could</u> (or <u>might</u>, <u>may</u>, <u>must</u>) improve in day-care centers.

Another very common sentence pattern can be used to express these meanings, and in fact express them with great exactness:

It is _____A_____ that _____B_____.

For example:

b.   It is <u>probable</u> that <u>children's social skills improve in day-care centers</u>.
      A   B

As you can see from this example, position A is filled with a word that expresses possibility, probability, or certainty. Position B is filled with a clause. This pattern is especially common in academic writing. The following are some of the words that can take position A in this pattern:

Possibility	Probability	Certainty
conceivable	probable	certain
possible	likely	obvious
		clear
negative probability { improbable		evident
{ unlikely		
		impossible } negative
		inconceivable } certainty

Exercise   *In the following exercise you are given content cues, that is, words that are intended to help you think up a sentence. In the first one, for example, you are intended to ask yourself what the effect of day care is on children. Your opinions may be quite different, and you may be quite certain or quite tentative about your opinions. Using the preceding pattern, write sentences expressing your opinions on the following situations and their possible effects. Note: You do not have to use the exact words given in the sentences you write.*

	Situation	**Effect on**
1.	day care	children

Ex: It is probable that children's social skills improve in day care.

(or)   It is clear that children receive less individual attention in day care than at home.

	Situation	**Effect on**
2.	declining marriage rate	birth rate
3.	divorce	children
4.	women's careers	marriage age
5.	later marriages	family size
6.	mothers' working	children

7. women's working   divorce rate

8. changing sexual morality   marriage rate

ADDITIONAL WRITING TOPICS

1. You saw that the number of mother-headed families increased between 1970 and 1983, primarily as a result of divorce. You might be interested in writing an essay on the financial status of such families. Here are some statistics to consider:

   In 1983 the median income for married-couple families was $27,286; the median income for mother-headed families was $11,789.

   In 1981 the average income for each member of a married-couple family was $8516; for each member of a mother-headed family it was $4530.

   In 1978 only 48.3% of women raising children by themselves were supposed to receive child support from the fathers of the children. And only 48.9% of these women received the full amount they were supposed to receive.*

   Here are some questions to think about: What is the financial effect of divorce? Why does a married-couple family have a much larger income? Why don't women earn more? What is the income for a family consisting of a husband, wife and one child? Of a family consisting of a mother and two children? Do most fathers not living with their families support their children? Do you think child support is more common among higher or lower income groups?

2. Write an essay giving your personal reaction to the changes in the American family that you have learned about in this lesson. This question is different from the others in asking for personal opinion, but it requires that you consider your opinions carefully before you begin writing. Which of these changes do you find negative and which might you find positive? Consider such things as the best age for marriage, the ideal family size, the importance of careers for women, the effects of women's working on children, the effects of divorce, the desirability of unmarried couples living together. You do not, of course, have to write on each of these topics; you may choose to narrow the topic.

3. The statistics in Table 8-2 show the percentages of foreign students enrolled in four fields of study in the United States in two different academic years, 1969–70 and 1981–82. As you can see, the percentages enrolled in these four fields are quite high. For example, in 1981–82 42.5 percent of all Middle Eastern students in the United States were studying engineering. Do you think these regional statistics accurately reflect what students from your country study in the United States? If so, why do students from your country

*(Sources: U.S. Bureau of the Census, *Current Population Reports*, P-60, No. 145, P-23, nos. 112 & 130.)

Table 8-2 Foreign Student Enrollment by Region and Field of Study: 1969/70 and 1981/82
(Non-immigrants Only)

REGION	FIELD OF STUDY (PERCENTAGES)			
	Engineering	Business/ Management	Physical Science	Math/ Computers
	69/70–81/2	69/70–81/2	69/70–81/2	69/70–81/2
Africa	16.0 16.5	11.7 24.8	13.5 7.2	2.2 3.5
Latin America	17.4 18.5	12.6 18.6	8.7 6.1	2.0 4.6
Middle East	36.4 42.5	9.2 12.5	10.6 6.4	3.2 6.8
South & East Asia	28.5 20.7	11.1 19.9	17.5 8.9	4.9 10.0

Source: Institute of International Education, New York, *Profiles: The Foreign Student in the United States,* 1983.

major in these fields and why do they come to the United States to study? Are
there any significant changes for your region between 1969–70 and 1981–
82? Can you explain them?

4. The statistics in Table 8-3 concern the U.S. budget in 1983. They show how
large portions of the budget were spent and the spending priorities of the
U.S. government. Write an essay giving your opinion on these priorities.
Should the United States spend more or less on defense, social security,
education, environment, scientific research, and so on? Note: Although the
percentages may vary a bit from year to year, the question of priorities remains the same.

Table 8-3 U.S. Budget Expenditures as Percentage
of Total 1983 Budget (est.)

1. Income Security (e.g. social security, government pensions)	35.1%
2. Defense	26.7%
3. Health	10.2%
4. Education, Training, Employment	3.3%
5. Natural Resources and Environment	1.5%
6. International Affairs	1.5%
7. General Science, Space, Technology	1.0%
8. Energy	.6%

Source: U.S. Office of Management and Budget, *The Budget of the United States
Government,* in *Statistical Abstract of the United States, 1984,* pg. 320.

5. Write an essay on government spending in your country. You may not have
any statistics but you may have an idea of relative spending, whether, for
example, more is spent on education or defense. (You may want to see if a
reference librarian can help you find some statistics.) Are there any areas in
which too much money is spent? Not enough? Remember that it is not possible to increase spending in all areas; you must make choices. Remember, also,
to make your explanations clear to an American reader, one who may not
understand all the needs and problems of your country.

Lesson Nine

RESEARCHING A TOPIC

Subject: Environmental Causes of Cancer

Contents:

INTRODUCTION

This lesson, which deals with the environmental causes of cancer, offers a thorough review of the ideas of cause and result introduced in the last lesson. The primary goal of the lesson, however, is to introduce you to the basics of library research. You will learn the basic conventions used in documenting and reporting on research, but more important, you will come to regard research as a process, one which includes narrowing down a topic, searching, reading, selecting, and finally reporting, or writing.

Cycle One consists of two rather short exercises designed to acquaint you with some of the questions that arise in discussing the environmental causes of cancer. The exercises will remind you of anything you may already know about the topic and help you decide which aspect of the problem you wish to research.

After choosing your research topic, you will be ready to continue on to Cycle Two, which will introduce you to two basic research tools, the card catalog and the *Reader's Guide to Periodical Literature*. This section also introduces the conventions of academic quotation and documentation. At this point you will be ready to go to the library and actually research your topic, which you will later report on orally to the rest of your research group. At the end of the section you will take a short "exam" on both the question you have researched yourself and the ones others have reported on.

Adding On provides more practice in organization and grammar, especially complex paragraph development and signal expressions.

CYCLE ONE

Practice 1. Discussion

The following quotations all have to do with the environmental causes of cancer. Each quotation is followed by one or more discussion questions. You may be able to answer many of the questions, but you may not know the answers to others. At this point the questions are more important than the answers: The answers can be found in the library. Note: You will be given the sources of these quotations in Practice 4, where they will be used in an exercise.

Quotations

a. "An estimated 80 to 90 percent of all cancers have been attributed to environment—diet, lifestyle and pollution."

Questions

How is "environment" defined in this quotation?

Do you know of any foods that have been related to cancer?

What is "lifestyle" and how can it be related to cancer?

b. "Environment is . . . the air you breathe, the culture you live in . . . the physical chemicals with which you come in contact, the diet."

Questions

How can culture affect health?

What are some of the ways we come into contact with chemicals?

Do you know of any chemicals that have been linked to cancer?

c. "Studies suggest that a general increase in consumption of fiber-rich cereals, vegetables, and fruits, and decrease in consumption of fat-rich products and excessive alcohol would be prudent."

Questions

According to this quotation, which of the following foods would be part of an "anticancer diet": ice cream, beer, wheat, carrots, steak, fish, brown bread, hot dogs?

Which of these foods does the average American prefer?

Do you know of any foods which contain chemicals?

How do chemicals get into food?

d. "The proportion of cancer deaths that we have tentatively attributed to occupational causes is about 4% of all U.S. cancer deaths."

Question

What is an "occupational cause" of cancer?

e. "Studies have identified more than 36 [industrial] substances as carcinogenic to humans."

Questions

Do you know of any industrial chemicals that cause cancer?

Do you know of any industries in which workers have a high risk of cancer?

How can people who are not industrial workers come into contact with such chemicals?

f. "Each day every one of us is exposed to hundreds of synthetic chemicals, scores of which are known to be carcinogenic in animals. For instance, "unintentional" pollutants find their way into our air, food, and water. . . . Some known carcinogens are spewed into the air by automobiles and coal-burning power plants. Potent pesticides coat most of our fresh fruit and vegetables."

Questions

How do carcinogenic chemicals get into the air?

How do they get into the food chain?

How can pollutants get into water?

What do industries do with chemical waste?

g. "It has been estimated that over 50,000 chemicals produced in significant quantities are currently used in commerce and close to 1,000 new chemicals are introduced each year. Only a small fraction of these . . . were tested for carcinogenicity or mutagenicity before their use."

Questions

Are all new chemicals tested for carcinogenicity before they are used?

Do we know exactly how many of the chemicals in use may be carcinogenic? Why not?

> h.   "Numerous studies of Japanese bomb survivors have reported an early epidemic of cancers."

Questions

Are atomic bombs the only source of radiation?

How else might we be exposed to radiation?

Practice 2. Narrowing the Topic

As you can see from the preceding quotations, the topic "environmental causes of cancer" is a very large one. For one thing, the word *environment* is defined very broadly in this context, including everything from the food we eat to the air we breathe. If you had found the quotations just discussed in the course of research, you would have realized you had too much information for a short paper. You would have decided to focus on just one part of the question, to narrow the topic. You might have decided, for example, to focus on the relation between diet and cancer.

In this lesson the work of narrowing down the topic is done for you. The following outline divides the environmental causes of cancer into two major categories and five more specific ones: diet, lifestyle, general chemical pollution, occupational exposure to carcinogens, radiation pollution. Organize into research teams of five persons, with each person responsible for researching *one* of these topics.

You have already learned a bit about the environmental causes of cancer from the quotations discussed at the beginning of the lesson, and you may have known something about the topic before you began this lesson. Use what you already know to fill out as much as possible of the following outline. This will give you some idea of the kind of thing to look for when you get to the library.

ENVIRONMENTAL CAUSES OF CANCER

    I.   Personal and Cultural "Environment"

        A.   Diet

            Ex: fatty foods, pesticides _____

Examples?   _____

        B.   Lifestyle

Proof?   Ex: smoking, drinking _____

Statistics?   _____

   II.   Pollution

        C.   General Chemical Pollution

            Ex: toxic waste _____

Examples?

    D.   Occupational Exposure to Carcinogens
            Ex: asbestos

Examples?

    E.   Radiation

Examples?   Ex: bombs, X-rays

Proof?

Remember that when you have finished researching your topic, you will report back to the other members of your group. They will not want to hear you read aloud an article you have found; your report will have to be a paraphrase or summary of your reading: To communicate, it will have to be in English everyone can understand. While you are actually in the library, however, you will not be working with the members of your original group. You will probably want to work with the other people who are researching the same topic as you. All the people working on diet, for example, will want to help each other.

CYCLE TWO

Practice 3. The Card Catalog and *Readers' Guide to Periodical Literature*

The card catalog and the *Readers' Guide to Periodical Literature* are two of the basic tools of library research. The card catalog contains information about books (and sometimes films, cassette recordings, and so on). The *Readers' Guide* lists information about magazine articles published in a given year.

    The information in the "card" catalog may be stored in different ways: on cards, on microfiche, on computer terminal. All the information in the catalog is in alphabetical order. Most books in the library will be listed three times, once by title, once by author, and once by subject matter. If you already know the name of the book you want or who wrote it, you can look it up under its title or the author's name. If, however, you do not have a specific book in mind, you can look under a general subject heading, for example, cancer. Under this heading you will find listed all the books the library has related to the subject of cancer.

    The magazine articles listed in the *Readers' Guide* are organized by subject area, for example, cancer. There is one volume for each year, and the information, again, is listed in alphabetical order.

    You should understand that the card catalog and the *Readers' Guide* are only two of the tools for doing research. There are a number of indexes to periodicals and journals that are more specialized and perhaps more appropriate to your field of study than the *Readers' Guide*. You should not hesitate to ask a reference librarian or a professor what index is most appropriate for a particular field or a particular paper.

    For our purposes here, however, the card catalog and the *Readers' Guide* will be adequate. They will introduce you to the process of research, the process of searching for, finding, and selecting relevant information. The research tools used may differ but the process itself does not vary.

Exercise A   *Figure 9-1 gives two sample cards from a card catalog. On the first one, the most important information is indicated. On the second, identify the same information yourself. For example, on the first the title is indicated; on the second you will find it.*

As you do the exercise you will see that a card contains a great deal of information. At this beginning stage of your research, however, it is not all

Figure 9-1

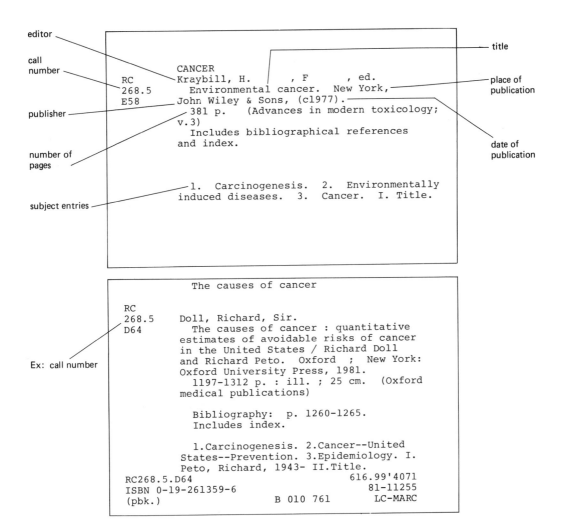

of equal importance. If you are looking under a subject heading such as CANCER, the first thing you must determine is whether a particular book is relevant to your topic. For example, a book on methods of treating cancer would be listed under CANCER but would not be relevant to the topic of environmental causes of cancer. Usually the title will be enough to indicate the general contents of a book. The titles of the two books in Figure 9-1 clearly indicate that they are relevant: *Environmental Cancer* and *The Causes of Cancer.* If the title is not as clear as these two, you can often get some idea of the contents by looking at the bottom of the card where other subject entries are given. Looking under the heading CANCER, you might find a book with the title *Malignant Neglect* and not be sure whether it would be helpful. At the bottom of the card you would find that it is also listed under the headings *carcinogenesis* and *environmentally induced diseases* and thus realize it is relevant.

If you decide you want to take a look at a particular book, you should note the call number (which is the code indicating where the book is stored), the title, and the author's name. Your teacher or a librarian will show you how to find a book using the call number.

At this point you do not need to note the other information contained on the card. Later in the lesson you will learn what information you will need to write a reference for a book you have used, but all this information can be gotten from the book itself.

Exercise B   *Study the sample pages from the* Readers' Guide *and then answer the questions which follow.*

To use the *Readers' Guide,* you would start with the most recent volume and look under the general heading CANCER. The general heading is often divided into subheadings. As you can see in Figure 9-2, the general heading CANCER is divided into these subheadings: *Causes, Diagnosis, Genetic aspects, Immunilogical aspects, Nutritional aspects, Prevention, Psychological aspects,* and *Statistics.* The subheadings *Causes* and *Nutritional aspects* are clearly the most relevant to your research topics. Under the general heading CANCER and most of the subheadings you will see the words *see also.* Listed under these words are other headings you might want to look under. For example, in the *see also* section under the subheading *Causes* you will see *Radiation—Physiological effects.* This means that if you look under the general heading RADIATION and the subheading *Physiological effects,* you might find articles discussing radiation as a cause of cancer.

When you have decided where to start looking, or which subheading is most relevant, begin reading the titles of the magazine articles listed. Sometimes a very brief description of the contents of an article is given after the title (see Figure 9-2). When you find an article that might be of interest, write down all the information you will need to find it: the name of the publication, the volume and page numbers, the date of publication. At this point you may need help to find the magazine, which may be stored on a shelf or on microfiche or microfilm; ask your teacher or a librarian.

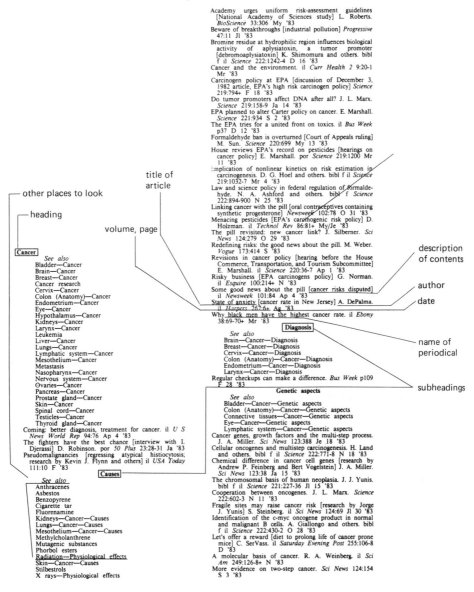

MARCH 1983 - FEBRUARY 1984   295

other places to look

heading

title of article

volume, page

Cancer
See also
Bladder—Cancer
Brain—Cancer
Breast—Cancer
Cancer research
Cervix—Cancer
Colon (Anatomy)—Cancer
Endometrium—Cancer
Eye—Cancer
Hypothalamus—Cancer
Kidneys—Cancer
Larynx—Cancer
Leukemia
Liver—Cancer
Lungs—Cancer
Lymphatic system—Cancer
Mesothelium—Cancer
Metastasis
Nasopharynx—Cancer
Nervous system—Cancer
Ovaries—Cancer
Pancreas—Cancer
Prostate gland—Cancer
Skin—Cancer
Spinal cord—Cancer
Testicles—Cancer
Thyroid gland—Cancer
Coming: better diagnosis, treatment for cancer. il U S News World Rep 94:76 Ap 4 '83
The fighters have the best chance [interview with I. Djerassi] D. Robinson. por 50 Plus 23:28-31 Ja 3 '83
Pseudomalignancies [regressing atypical histiocytosis; research by Kevin J. Flynn and others] il USA Today 111:10 F '83

Causes
See also
Anthracenes
Asbestos
Benzopyrene
Cigarette tar
Fluorenamine
Kidneys—Cancer—Causes
Lungs—Cancer—Causes
Mesothelium—Cancer—Causes
Methylcholanthrene
Mutagenic substances
Phorbol esters
Radiation—Physiological effects
Skin—Cancer—Causes
Stilbestrols
X rays—Physiological effects

Academy urges uniform risk-assessment guidelines [National Academy of Sciences study] L. Roberts. BioScience 33:306 My '83
Beware of breakthroughs [industrial pollution] Progressive 47:11 Jl '83
Bromine residue at hydrophilic region influences biological activity of aplysiatoxin, a tumor promoter [debromoaplysiatoxin] K. Shimomura and others. bibl f il Science 222:1242-4 D 16 '83
Cancer and the environment. il Curr Health 2 9:20-1 Mr '83
Carcinogen policy at EPA [discussion of December 3, 1982 article, EPA's high risk carcinogen policy] Science 219:794+ F 18 '83
Do tumor promoters affect DNA after all? J. L. Marx. Science 219:158-9 Ja 14 '83
EPA planned to alter Carter policy on cancer. E. Marshall. Science 221:934 S 2 '83
The EPA tries for a united front on toxics. il Bus Week p37 D 12 '83
Formaldehyde ban is overturned [Court of Appeals ruling] M. Sun. Science 220:699 My 13 '83
House reviews EPA's record on pesticides [hearings on cancer policy] E. Marshall. por Science 219:1200 Mr 11 '83
:mplication of nonlinear kinetics on risk estimation in carcinogenesis. D. G. Hoel and others. bibl f il Science 219:1032-7 Mr 4 '83
Law and science policy in federal regulation of formaldehyde. N. A. Ashford and others. bibl f Science 222:894-900 N 25 '83
Linking cancer with the pill [oral contraceptives containing synthetic progesterone] Newsweek 102:78 O 31 '83
Menacing pesticides [EPA's carcinogenic risk policy] D. Holzman. il Technol Rev 86:81+ My/Je '83
The pill revisited: new cancer link? J. Silberner. Sci News 124:279 O 29 '83
Redefining risks: the good news about the pill. M. Weber. Vogue 173:414 S '83
Revisions in cancer policy [hearing before the House Commerce, Transportation, and Tourism Subcommittee] E. Marshall. il Science 220:36-7 Ap 1 '83
Risky business [EPA carcinogens policy] G. Norman. il Esquire 100:214+ N '83
Some good news about the pill [cancer risks disputed] il Newsweek 101:84 Ap 4 '83
State of anxiety [cancer rate in New Jersey] A. DePalma. il Harpers 267:6+ Ag '83
Why black men have the highest cancer rate. il Ebony 38:69-70+ Mr '83

Diagnosis
See also
Brain—Cancer—Diagnosis
Breast—Cancer—Diagnosis
Cervix—Cancer—Diagnosis
Colon (Anatomy)—Cancer—Diagnosis
Endometrium—Cancer—Diagnosis
Larynx—Cancer—Diagnosis
Regular checkups can make a difference. Bus Week p109 F 28 '83

Genetic aspects
See also
Bladder—Cancer—Genetic aspects
Colon (Anatomy)—Cancer—Genetic aspects
Connective tissues—Cancer—Genetic aspects
Eye—Cancer—Genetic aspects
Lymphatic system—Cancer—Genetic aspects
Cancer genes, growth factors and the multi-step process. J. A. Miller. Sci News 123:388 Je 18 '83
Cellular oncogenes and multistep carcinogenesis. H. Land and others. bibl f il Science 222:771-8 N 18 '83
Chemical difference in cancer cell genes [research by Andrew P. Feinberg and Bert Vogelstein] J. A. Miller. Sci News 123:38 Ja 15 '83
The chromosomal basis of human neoplasia. J. J. Yunis. bibl f il Science 221:227-36 Jl 15 '83
Cooperation between oncogenes. J. L. Marx. Science 222:602-3 N 11 '83
Fragile sites may raise cancer risk [research by Jorge J. Yunis] S. Steinberg. il Sci News 124:69 Jl 30 '83
Identification of the c-myc oncogene product in normal and malignant B cells. A. Giallongo and others. bibl f il Science 222:430-2 O 28 '83
Let's offer a reward [diet to prolong life of cancer prone mice] C. SerVass. il Saturday Evening Post 255:106-8 D '83
A molecular basis of cancer. R. A. Weinberg. il Sci Am 249:126-8+ N '83
More evidence on two-step cancer. Sci News 124:154 S 3 '83

description of contents

author

date

name of periodical

subheadings

Figure 9-2

Cancer—Genetic aspects—*cont.*

Mutation affecting the 12th amino acid of the c-Ha-ras oncogene product occurs infrequently in human cancer. A. P. Feinberg and others. bibl f il *Science* 220:1175-7 Je 10 '83

Normal cells of patients with high cancer risk syndromes lack transforming activity in the NIH/3T3 transfection assay. S. W. Needleman and others. bibl f il *Science* 222:173-5 O 14 '83

Of mice and men [diet research to prolong lives of mice who have cancer genes] C. SerVaas. il *Saturday Evening Post* 255:106-8 N '83

Oncogenetic switch. *Sci Am* 248:73 Ap '83

Predisposition test [cancer linked to fragile sites on chromosomes; research by Jorge J. Yunis] *USA Today* 112:11-12 O '83

The search for the origins of cancer. R. A. Weinberg. il *Technol Rev* 86:46-53+ O '83

Transformation of Bloom's syndrome fibroblasts by DNA transfection. J. Doniger and others. bibl f il *Science* 222:1144-6 D 9 '83

Immunological aspects

See also

Breast—Cancer—Immunological aspects

Lymphatic system—Cancer—Immunological aspects

Skin—Cancer—Immunological aspects ⟶ — relevant subheading

| Nutritional aspects |

See also

Cervix—Cancer—Nutritional aspects

Colon (Anatomy)—Cancer—Nutritional aspects

Leukemia—Nutritional aspects

Lymphatic system—Cancer—Nutritional aspects

At last, an anti-cancer diet. W. S. Ross. *Read Dig* 122:78-82 F '83

Can vitamins help prevent cancer? [report by National Research Council] il *Consum Rep* 48:243-5 My '83

Cancer and cuisine [views of Bruce N. Ames] S. Steinberg. il *Sci News* 124:217 O 1 '83

Diet, nutrition & cancer. M. Mercer. il *Good Housekeep* 196:83-6+ F '83

Dietary carcinogens and anticarcinogens [with editorial comment by Philip H. Abelson] B. N. Ames. bibl f *Science* 221:1249, 1256-64 S 23 '83

Let's offer a reward [diet to prolong life of cancer prone mice] C. SerVass. il *Saturday Evening Post* 255:106-8 D '83

Lysine experiment in Budapest [cancer experiment] C. SerVaas. *Saturday Evening Post* 255:106 D '83

Lysine for herpes update. C. SerVaas. *Saturday Evening Post* 255:106-7 My/Je '83

Of mice and men [diet research to prolong lives of mice who have cancer genes] C. SerVaas. il *Saturday Evening Post* 255:106-8 N '83

Phenomena, comment and notes [views of B. N. Ames on dietary carcinogens and anticarcinogens] J. P. Wiley, Jr. *Smithsonian* 14:38+ N '83

Reduce cancer risk. *Blair Ketchums Ctry J* 10:17-18 F '83

Seeds of hope [protease inhibitors in edible seeds prevent cancer; work of Walter Troll and others] B. M. Ribakove. il *Health* 15:12 Ag '83

Tracing cancer to diet. il *Consum Res Mag* 66:27-9 Mr '83

The truth about cancer and what you eat. il *Changing Times* 37:39-42 Jl '83

What we really know about diet and cancer. W. A. Nolen. il *McCalls* 110:82+ My '83

Prevention

See also

Cancer inhibiting substances

Skin—Cancer—Prevention

Cancer: cutting the risks. il *Bus Week* p156-7+ F 14 '83

Psychological aspects

See also

Breast—Cancer—Psychological aspects

Cancer phobia

Video victory over cancer? [Killer T-Cell] il *Sci Dig* 91:87 Je '83

Statistics

Beating cancer—odds improve. il *U S News World Rep* 95:13 D 12 '83

Figure 9-2 continued

Questions

1. Which of the headings listed under *see also* under the subheading *Causes* might be useful to members of your research group?

2. What is the article "Beware of Breakthroughs" (under *Causes*) about? What magazine was it published in? What date? What page is it on? Is the author given?

3. Which article (under *Causes*) has the word "Environment" in its title? What magazine is it in? What date?

4. Which articles (under *Causes*) deal with pesticides?

5. Would articles on birth control pills and cancer be relevant to anyone in your research group?
6. Who wrote "Cancer and Cuisine" (under *Nutritional aspects*)? What is this article about?
7. Are there any articles about smoking or radiation under the subheadings *Causes* and *Nutritional aspects*?

Practice 4. Documenting an Essay

In a piece of writing, any idea or information which is not your own or not common knowledge must be documented; that is, you must give the source of the information; you must tell the reader where you got it. In doing research on cancer, for example, you might read that smoking is related to cancer; you would not need to document this, however, because it is common knowledge. On the other hand, if you find and use a statistic on the relation between smoking and cancer you will have to provide the source: The statistic is not your own and it is not common knowledge.

Before studying the details of documentation, there are two general points you should understand. First, the *purpose* of documentation is to give the reader all the information necessary to go to the library and *find* the information you have used. Errors of punctuation, capitalization, and so on, are minor ones, but any error that makes it impossible to find your source easily is a major one.

Second, in this lesson you will learn only one of the several methods of documenting a source: the author-date-page system as given in the *MLA Handbook for Writers of Research Papers,* Second Edition. You may wish to consult this book, which your library will surely have, for more detail. If your teacher prefers another system of documentation, such as the footnoting method, use that method. The important thing at this point is to learn one method well and not to mix different systems: one method is as good as another.

The Author-Date-Page System.   To document a source you must do two things. You must indicate which ideas in your essay are taken from your reading and then, at the end of the essay, tell where you got them. The details of documentation can become quite complex, but the basic idea, as you can see from the following example, is clear enough:

> a. Diet is related to cancer in a number of ways. Some of the pesticides used in growing food and some of the chemicals added in processing food are carcinogenic (Gonzales 1976, 72). Some of these chemicals are added to improve the flavor of food, others, such as sodium nitrate, to make it last longer on the shelf, and others, such as food dyes, to make it look better. It is an oversimplification, however, to think that only man-made chemicals can cause cancer. Researchers have found that a number of entirely natural substances are carcinogenic (Ames 1983, 1,256–59). Such natural substances as alcohol and animal fat have been associated with certain types of cancer. Even some compounds found in pepper,

celery, fava beans, and cottonseed, to name a few foods, may be carcinogenic. At the same time a number of naturally occurring substances such as vitamin E, carotene, ascorbic acid, and uric acid are thought to be anticarcinogens (Ames 1983, 1,259–60). A natural but balanced diet is therefore the healthiest diet.

References

Ames, Bruce N. 1983. "Dietary Carcinogens and Anticarcinogens." *Science* 23 Sept: 1,256–63.

Gonzales, Nicholas. 1976. "Preventing Cancer." *Family Health/Health Today* May: 30+.

In this example you can see that ideas taken from reading are identified by the information in parentheses: the author's last name, the year of publication, and the relevant pages. The reader can find the source fully identified in the list of references at the end of the paper. This example can be used to make a second important point: You do not have to document every sentence (even if every sentence is based on your reading) provided that the reader can tell where you got your information. The sentence stating that some pesticides and additives are carcinogenic is documented (Gonzales 1976, 72) but the following sentence giving examples of additives is not: It is clear from the context that this information, too, is from Gonzales. Similarly, all the information concerning natural carcinogens is from Ames although only the first sentence dealing with this topic is documented. The Ames article is referred to a second time, however, in connection with the idea of natural *anti*carcinogens because it is not obvious that this idea is from the same source. Document as much as necessary to be clear and honest, but use common sense—the reader will too.

As you have just seen, the question of documentation can be divided into two parts: the parenthetical information in the body of the essay and the list of references at the end. The following explanation follows that division.

Parenthetical Information.　The parenthetical information may consist of the author's name, the year, and the relevant pages and be placed at the end of the sentence, just before the period:

> b.　Researchers have found that a number of entirely natural substances are carcinogenic (Ames 1983, 1,256–59).

At times, however, the end of the sentence is not the most natural position for the parenthetical information:

> c.　According to some experts (Ames 1983, 1,256), we should eat a diet rich in cereals, vegetables, and fruits.

If the author's name is mentioned in the sentence, it is not necessary to repeat it in parentheses. In the following example notice also that the author Ames is identified for a reader with no special knowledge of the field.

    d.   Bruce N. Ames, the chairperson of the Department of Biochemistry at the University of California, Berkeley, advises that we should eat a diet rich in cereals, vegetables, and fruits (1983, 1,256).

It is not necessary to give a page number if you are referring to an idea that is developed throughout an entire article or book:

    e.   In an important article, Ames (1983) explains that the average diet consists of both natural carcinogens and anticarcinogens.

Finally, if you are documenting an article for which no author is given, put the title of the article (or a shortened form of the title) in parentheses:

    f.   Some scientists believe that 80–90% of all cancers are due to the environment, in the broadest sense of that word ("Environmental Cancer" 1980, 5).

"Environmental Cancer" is a shortened form of "Environmental Cancer on the Rise"; it would not be possible to shorten it to "Cancer on the Rise" because in the list of references the article would be alphabetized under the first important word, "Environmental."

The List of References.   All the sources that you have referred to in your essay are listed, in alphabetical order, at the end of the paper under the heading *References*. The sources are alphabetized according to the author's last name, or if the author's name is not given, the first important word in the title. The following sample list of references will show you how to document four of the most common sources: a book, a collection (a book which consists of articles by different writers), a magazine, and a professional or academic journal. For your convenience these are labeled; you would not normally label the entries in a list of references. A discussion follows these examples:

References

Book:	Doll, Richard, and Richard Peto. 1981. *The Causes of Cancer: Quantitative Estimates of Avoidable Risks of Cancer in the United States.* New York: Oxford UP.
Magazine:	"Environmental Cancer on the Rise." 1980. *Science News* 5 July: 5.
Collection:	Furst, Arthur. 1977. "Inorganic Agents as Carcinogens." *Environmental Cancer.* Ed. H. F. Kraybill and Myron A. Mehlman. New York: Wiley & Sons. 209–29.
Journal:	Senie, Ruby Tomberg, Paul Peter Rosen, and David W. Kinne. 1983. "Epidemilogic Factors Associated with Breast Cancer." *Cancer Nursing* 6: 367–71.

As you can see from these examples, the basic form for a reference is:

Author(s). Year. "Title of Article or Essay." *Title of Book or Publication.* Editor or translator. Publishing information. Pages.

As much of this information as is available is given, though often you will not have all this information: The author's name may not be given; your source may not be an article; there may be no editor or translator. Simply include as much of the above information as you do have. The information is given in the order just indicated, with one possible exception: If there is no author's name, do not begin with the year; always place the year in the second position.

The following provides somewhat more detail on the elements of the basic reference.

Author(s).   The family name of the author precedes the given name. If there is more than one author, the names of all but the first are written in the normal order, given name preceding family name: <u>Doll, Richard, and Richard Peto.</u>

Year.   In this system the year of publication is placed right after the author's name. If you happen to refer to two publications by the same author in the same year, use letters to distinguish them in both your essay and your list of references: (Ames 1983<u>a</u>) and Ames 1983<u>b</u>). If you refer to two publications by the same author in different years, list the earlier one first.

Title of Article or Essay.   If you are referring to a part of a publication (an article, an essay, a chapter), that information is placed right after the year. This type of title is punctuated with quotation marks; the first word and all other principal words are capitalized: "<u>E</u>nvironmental <u>C</u>ancer on the <u>R</u>ise."

Title of Book or Publication.   The title of a book, magazine, journal, newspaper, or other publication is underlined with the first and all principal words capitalized: <u>Cancer Nursing.</u>

Editor or Translator.   The name of the editor or translator, if the work has been edited or translated, follows the title. Editor(s) is abbreviated <u>Ed.</u> and Translator(s) is abbreviated <u>Trans.</u> The given precedes the family name: <u>Ed. H. F. Kraybill and Myron A. Mehlman.</u>

Publishing Information.   At this point a reference for a book and a reference for a periodical become rather different. For a book give the city and the name of the publishing company, separated by a colon: <u>New York: Oxford UP.</u> If several cities are mentioned, just give the first one. For a magazine the date (except for the year) follows right after the title of the publication: <u>Science News 5 July:.</u> The date is sufficient for a magazine; it is not necessary to give the volume and issue number. On the other hand, for a journal with continuous pagination for a whole year, it is enough to give just the volume number: <u>Cancer Nursing 6:.</u> If, however, the journal does not have continuous pagination (if each issue begins with page 1), give both the volume and the issue number: <u>Bulletin of Environmental Contamination and Toxicology 17-2:.</u>

Pages.   In your essay you have already given in parentheses the specific page(s) you have drawn on. In the list of references it is not necessary to give the number of pages in a book (see the reference for *Causes of Cancer*), but you must give the pages for all articles, whether in a book or periodical. The punctuation is slightly different for books and periodicals. For an article in a book place a period after the publishing information and then give the pages; for a periodical place a colon after the date (magazine) or volume number (journal) and give the pages.

By now you probably feel that the conventions of documentation are extremely complicated. They are. The presentation here is quite simplified: There are whole books on the subject. Remember the basic rule—give the reader the information necessary to go to the library and find your source quickly. Do not be afraid to ask a teacher or a librarian for help, or best of all, learn how to use one of the reference works on the subject. In a week you will not remember what you have just read; be sure you know how to find it again when you need it.

Exercise   *At the beginning of this lesson you were given eight quotations concerning cancer. The eight sources in this exercise relate to those quotations: Source 1 below, for example, provides the information necessary to write a reference for quotation **a** at the beginning. But this information does not follow the conventions you have been studying. Use this information to write a correct list of references.*

1. Name of magazine: science news; title of article: environmental cancer on the rise; page: 5; date: 5 July 1980; author: not given.

Ex: "Environmental Cancer on the Rise." 1980. Science News 5 July: 5.

2. Date: 28 Sept., 1979; title of article: cancer and the environment: Higginson speaks out; name of magazine: science; author: not given; pages: 1,363–66.

3. Author: Bruce N. Ames; title of article: dietary carcinogens and anticarcinogens; date: 23 Sept., 1983; name of magazine: science; pages: 1,256–64.

4. Title of book: the causes of cancer: quantitative estimates of avoidable risks of cancer in the united states; date: 1981; authors: Richard Doll and Richard Peto; publisher: Oxford University Press; place: New York.

5. Author: Devra Lee Davis; name of magazine: environment; title of article: cancer in the workplace: the case for prevention; date: July/August 1981; pages: 25–37.

6. Date: May, 1976; author: Nicholas Gonzales; title of article: preventing cancer; name of magazine: family health/health today; pages: 30+.

7. Title of pamphlet (book): environmental chemicals causing cancer and genetic birth defects: developing a strategy to minimize human exposure; author: Bruce N. Ames; date: 1978; publisher: Institute of Governmental Studies; place: Berkeley.

8. Author: J. Raloff; title of article: a-bomb survivor risks are revised upward; magazine: science news; page: 405; date: 19 June 1982.

Practice 5. Academic Quotation

In a paper based on reading you may want to use direct quotation; but be careful not to overuse it: paraphrase is the basic method of reporting information. Direct quotation should be used for special effect, for variety, or because an idea is expressed especially well in the original. Quotation should never be used because it is easier to write than good paraphrase. The following paragraph, for example, is based on quotations at the beginning of the lesson, but direct quotation is used only once, at the end, to give the concluding point special emphasis:

a. One of the most important types of environmental pollution is chemical pollution, both in the general environment and at the workplace. As many as 36 industrial substances, for example, are known to be carcinogenic (Davis 1981, 27). The problem is serious and affects all of us. As one writer puts it, "Each day every one of us is exposed to hundreds of synthetic chemicals, scores of which are known to be carcinogens in animals" (Gonzales 1976, 72).

There are a number of points to note about direct quotation. First, direct quotation is always documented. Second, there are a number of conventions of punctuation and capitalization to follow. A quotation is usually separated from the introductory part of the sentence by a comma, and the first word of the quotation is capitalized, if the quotation would be a complete sentence by itself, as in example *a* above. However, no comma or capitalization is used if the quotation is grammatically integrated into the rest of the sentence, as in example b, or would not be a complete sentence if it stood by itself, as in example *c*:

b. In an article on the prevention of cancer Gonzales (1976, 72) says <u>that</u> "each day every one of us is exposed to hundreds of synthetic chemicals."

c. The environment may be defined as "the air you breathe, the culture you live in . . . the physical chemicals with which you come in contact, the diet" ("Cancer and the Environment" 1979, 1363).

In these last two examples you can also see that the final period is placed inside the closing quotation marks (example *b*) unless the sentence closes with parenthetical documentation (example *c*).

Next, you should take care to fit quotations smoothly into your writing, using only as much as you need to make your point. You may be able to paraphrase part of the original, giving only the main idea in direct quotation. You may leave some words out of the original; these cuts are indicated by dots (. . .). Or, to make a quotation clear in the context of your writing, you might add a word or two to the original; any additions are enclosed in brackets ([ ]). Compare the full quote given below in example *d* with the partial quote in example *e,* which makes use of paraphrase, dots and brackets:

d. "Studies suggest that a general increase in consumption of fiber-rich cereals, vegetables, and fruits, and decrease in consumption of fat-rich products and excessive alcohol would be prudent."

e. In an article in <u>Science</u> (1983, 1256) Ames advises us to eat more "fiber-rich cereals, vegetables and fruits and . . . [fewer] fat-rich products."

The original *studies suggest that a general increase in consumption of* in d is paraphrased as *Ames advises us to eat more* in e. The dots in e indicate that something has been left out of the middle of the quote (the words *decrease in consumption of*). It is not necessary to indicate that words are left off the beginning or the end of a quotation. The brackets in e indicate that the word *fewer* has been added.

Finally, it is usually best to introduce a direct quotation. One common pattern of introduction is *"according to X"*: *"According to Bruce N. Ames . . . ",* *"According to an article in **Science** . . .".* Another pattern is *"X says (shows, points out, argues," and so on):* *"Ames advises . . .", "An article in **Scientific American** shows . . .",* *"A government study indicates . . .".* When introducing quotations be careful to avoid fragments:

f. *According to Bruce N. Ames, "more fiber-rich cereals, vegetables and fruits."

In summary: Do not overquote; document all quotations; fit quotations smoothly into your writing; introduce most quotations.

Exercise   *Use the information in the following quotation to answer the questions in this exercise. Include quotations in your answers. Introduce the quotations and be sure their meaning is clear.*

Smoking increases the death rate to an alarming degree. It encourages hardening of the arteries. It doubles the heart attack rate. It increases the emphysema rate by at least four times. And it increases the lung cancer rate by as much as twenty times. It also increases the chances of developing many other diseases.

In the age group 45–64, nonsmokers die at an annual rate of 708 persons per 100,000 population. Smokers die at the rate of 1329 persons per 100,000 population. Of these, heart disease accounts for 615 of the smokers' deaths, 304 of the nonsmokers' deaths. Lung cancer accounts for 87 deaths for smokers and 11 for nonsmokers. Emphysema accounts for 24 of smokers' deaths and 4 of nonsmokers' deaths. [Robert O'Connor. 1980. *Choosing for Health.* Philadelphia: Saunders College/Holt. 137.]

1. What is the relation between smoking and emphysema?

Ex: O'Connor (1980, 137) reports that smoking is directly related to emphysema. Every year for every 100,000 people in the 45–64 age group, "Emphysema accounts for 24 of smokers' deaths and 4 of nonsmokers' deaths."

Ex: Smoking is directly related to emphysema. Indeed, according to studies of the death rate (O'Connor 1980, 137), "It increases the emphysema rate by at least four times."

2. What is the relation between smoking and the death rate?

3. What is the relation between smoking and deaths from heart disease?

4. What is the relation between smoking and death from lung cancer?

Practice 6. Oral Report and Directed Writing:
The Environmental Causes of Cancer

While researching your topic, it will probably be best to take reading notes on information you think important (see Lesson 5, Practice 4 & 7). If you work from notes you will be forced to use summary and paraphrase when you report to the other members of your group and when you write on your topic. If you find something you may want to use as a quotation, copy it down carefully. Remember that both paraphrased information and quotations must be documented; be sure to write down all the information you will need to write a list of references.

When you have finished your research, give your oral reports and work together on the following "exam." To answer the first short-answer questions you will have to rely on the information provided by other members of your group in their oral reports. For the longer essay question you will probably choose to write on the topic you researched yourself.

Short-Answer Questions
1. Contrast a healthy diet with one that increases the risk of getting cancer.
2. How are smoking and drinking related to cancer?
3. What are some kinds of environmental pollution which have been linked to cancer?
4. Give examples of occupational cancer risks.
5. How do we know that cancer is related to radiation?

Essay Question
Answer one of the preceding questions at greater length, being careful to support and explain your ideas adequately. Use quotation and especially paraphrase, making parenthetical reference to your sources and providing a list of references at the end.

ADDING ON

Practice 7. Complex Paragraph Development

In each lesson in this book you have practiced at least one or two ways to organize and develop paragraphs. In advanced writing, these methods of organizing and developing ideas are most often mixed. The following short essay is an example of mixed, or complex, development. The logical relations (or methods of organizing and developing) are given in parentheses:

	LOGICAL RELATION
CONTROLLING CANCER	
1 There are two main causes of cancer: heredity and environment. We can do nothing to change our heredity, that	(*Division.*)
is, the basic physical characteristics that were passed on to us by	(*Definition.*)
our parents. However, we can do a great deal to control our	(*Contrast.*)
5 environment, which may account for 80–90% of all cancers	(*Statistic.*)
("Environmental Cancer" 1980, 5).	
Environmental pollution can be divided into two kinds:	(*Division.*)
personal and impersonal. Personal pollution may be defined	(*Definition.*)
roughly as unhealthy habits such as smoking, drinking, and	(*Examples.*)
10 eating the wrong foods. Clearly, with enough will power we	
can control this personal environment.	
Impersonal pollution, on the other hand, refers to	(*Contrast.*)
those things which are beyond our individual control. One	(*Definition.*)
example would be industrial pollution, which is very hard to	(*Example.*)
15 control because of the expense involved. It would be expensive	(*Cause.*)
in terms of profits and perhaps jobs. The American auto-	(*Restatement.*)
mobile industry, for example, resisted the law requiring smog-	(*Example.*)
control devices because it feared the added expense would	
reduce profits. Nevertheless, some laws protecting the envi-	(*Concession.*)
20 ronment have been quite successful in reducing pollution.	

Reference

"Environmental Cancer on the Rise." 1980. *Science News* 5 July: 5.

Exercise   *The following paragraphs are inadequately developed. Developing material might be added where indicated by the blanks. Following each paragraph are questions that will help you decide what kind of information to add. The first one, in the first paragraph, is done as an example.*

1.   Many of the chemicals which we add to our foods have been linked to cancer. One writer refers to these chemicals as "intentional" pollutants (Gonzales 1976, 72). The flavor enhancers, preservatives, and colorings we add can all be thought of as "intentional" pollutants. ___(a)___. Some have been shown to cause cancer in laboratory animals. ___(b)___.

Reference

Gonzales, Nicholas. 1976. "Preventing Cancer." *Family Health/Health Today* May: 30+.

a.   Can you *restate* or explain what is meant by the term "intentional" pollutant? What do flavor enhancers, preservatives, and colorings do?

b.   Can you add an *example* or two of a food additive that has been linked to cancer?

Ex: Many of the chemicals which we add to our foods have been linked to cancer. One writer refers to these chemicals as "intentional" pollutants (Gonzales 1976, 72). In other words, we add these pollutants on purpose, because we want our food to look better, last longer, and taste better. . . .

2.   The chemicals used in industry are dangerous to both the workers in certain industries and the general public, which is exposed to the carcinogens contained in industrial wastes and by-products. _____(a)_____ _____. Some progress has been made in reducing industrial pollution, but it is difficult to control because of the political pressure exerted by special industrial interests. ___(b)___ _____. One example of such an industrial interest is the meat-packing industry, which resists limitations on the use of nitrates in packaged meats.

a.   Did anyone in your research group find *examples* of industrial carcinogens?

b.   Can you *restate* this idea? How can an industry be politically powerful?

3.   We consider ourselves lucky to be able to afford a rich and varied diet. An American might eat a greater variety of foods in one day than a peasant in a poor country in a year. _____(a)_____ _____. But in a sense it is also our wealth that makes it possible to eat an unhealthy diet. Many of the things Americans like to eat have been linked to cancer. _____(b)_____ _____.

a.   Can you add a sentence listing what a typical American might eat in a day?

b. What *examples* did you find of foods that Americans like which are related to cancer?

4. Exposure to radiation is known to be related to cancer. Survivors of Hiroshima and Nagasaki have had a much higher incidence of cancer than the rest of the Japanese population. _____(a)_____ _____. Weapons testing has also been linked to some kinds of cancer. _____(b)_____ _____. Nuclear weapons, however, are not the only sources of radiation in the modern world. _____(c)_____ _____.

a. Can you *restate* this idea emphatically beginning with the word *indeed* and using quotation h from the beginning of the lesson, which speaks of an "epidemic of cancers"? Did anyone find a *statistic* to support this idea?

b. Did anyone find an *example* of this? Did anyone find a *statistic* to support this idea?

c. What are some other sources of radiation that have been linked to cancer?

Practice 8. Cause/Result Signals

In Lesson 8, Practice 5, you were introduced to these *cause/result signals: because, since, therefore, consequently, for this reason, as a result, because of, due to, as a result of, reason for, cause of.* The following examples summarize the use of these signals:

a. The cancer rate in big cities may be higher than in the country <u>because</u> there is more pollution.

b. There is more pollution in big cities than in the country; <u>therefore</u>, city dwellers may have a greater risk of getting cancer.

c. The cancer rate is high in big cities partly <u>because of</u> urban pollution.

d. One of the <u>causes of</u> the high cancer rate in big cities may be pollution.

The relationship of cause and result can be signaled in a number of other ways, as well. A number of verb constructions, for example, may express cause and result. In the two following examples pay special attention to the prepositions that follow some of the verbs:

e. Industrial pollution <u>causes</u> a variety of health problems.
(or <u>brings about</u>, <u>creates</u>, <u>contributes to</u>, <u>results in</u>)

f. Industrial pollution <u>is related to</u> a variety of health problems.
(or <u>is connected to</u>, <u>is linked to</u>, <u>is responsible for</u>)

Finally, you have seen that the colon (:) can be used to introduce a list. It is sometimes also used to introduce either a cause or a result:

g. The American cancer rate is high<u>:</u> The American diet is carcinogenic in many ways.

h. The American diet is carcinogenic in many ways: The American cancer rate is high.

Exercise Write sentences of cause and result using the ideas suggested by the cues and the signal given in parentheses. In the cues you are given just enough words to suggest the idea. To produce a grammatical sentence you may have to change and add words.

	Cause	**Result**	
1.	dangerous chemicals	some workers . . . high cancer rate	(because of)

Ex: Because of the dangerous chemicals used in certain indus-tries, some workers have especially high cancer rates.
or Because of exposure to carcinogenic chemicals, workers in some industries have high cancer rates.

2.	vinyl chloride . . . manufac-turing rubber	rubber workers . . . cancer	(as a result)
3.	some preservatives	cancer in laboratory animals	(related to)
4.	pesticides increase agricultural production	hard to decrease use	(because)
5.	Northeast U.S. . . . heavily industrial	higher cancer rate than other areas	(therefore)
6.	food . . . spoil without pre-servatives	food industry resists removing them	(since)
7.	low-fat diet	Japanese have a low cancer rate	(as a result of)
8.	smoking	lung cancer	(due to)

9. pipe smoking   lip cancer   (linked to)

10. X-rays . . . radiation   used carefully   (:)

11. some industrial wastes . . . car-   disposed of carefully   (consequently)
     cinogenic

Practice 9. Concession Signals

In the section on complex paragraph development (Practice 7), you may have noticed that the last logical relation in the sample essay was marked *concession.* Concession signals indicate that the relation between two ideas is somewhat surprising or unexpected:

> a. Industrial pollution is very hard to control because of the expense involved. <u>Nev-</u>
>   <u>ertheless,</u> some laws protecting the environment have been quite successful in
>   reducing pollution.

Because pollution control is very expensive, we might *expect* that very little has been done; the second sentence, however, tells us that this is not true. To give another example, we might expect almost everyone to quit smoking because it is closely linked to lung cancer. We might be surprised that more people do not quit:

> b. <u>Although</u> cigarette smoking is the main cause of lung cancer, many people con-
>   tinue to smoke.

These examples consist of two parts, a situation and a counterexpectation, that is, the unexpected or surprising element. In the last example, the situation is the relation between smoking and cancer, and the counterexpectation is the fact that people continue smoking. Notice that the *noncombining signal nevertheless* is placed in the structure expressing counterexpectation, whereas the *combining signals (although, even though, though)* introduce the structure expressing the background situation:

> c. <u>Even though it is dangerous,</u> people continue to smoke.
> d. It is dangerous; <u>nevertheless, people continue to smoke.</u>

The word *yet* can also introduce the counterexpectation. *Yet* joins clauses. If they are short, as in the following example, no punctuation is necessary; if they are longer, they are usually separated by a comma:

e. It is dangerous <u>yet people continue to smoke.</u>

The expressions *despite* and *in spite of* may also be used to introduce the background situation. Notice that they must be followed by a noun structure or one that can function as a noun, such as a gerund:

f. <u>Despite the danger,</u> people continue to smoke.

g. <u>In spite of its causing lung cancer,</u> people continue to smoke.

Notice that contrast signals, *however* for example, can often be used to signal concession:

h. Smoking is dangerous; <u>however, people continue to smoke.</u>

It is not, however, possible to use concession signals to introduce a contrast which contains no element of surprise or unexpectedness. The following sentence, for example, would not make sense:

i. *Although Ming speaks Chinese, Hussein does not.

It is not surprising that Hussein does not speak Chinese: He is not Chinese.

Exercise *Use the concession signals given in parentheses to make the relation between the following ideas clear. You may have to change some words, as in the first example, to produce a grammatical sentence.*

1. Reducing pollution is expensive. Many countries have successfully reduced pollution. (despite)

Ex: <u>Despite the cost,</u> many countries have successfully reduced pollution.

2. Nitrates are carcinogenic. It is permitted to put them in packaged meats. (although)

Ex: <u>Although nitrates are carcinogenic,</u> it is permitted to put them in packaged meats.

3. Fish is better for the health than red meat. Americans prefer meat. (yet)

4. Beef is very high in fat. Beef is the favorite meat of most Americans. (in spite of)

5. The American diet is not especially healthy. Many American foods are becoming popular in other countries. (even though)

6. Pipe smoking is less dangerous than cigarette smoking. It is linked to lip cancer. (nevertheless)

7. It is difficult. Millions of people have quite smoking. (despite)

8. They are exposed to carcinogens. Some workers prefer the unsafe conditions to the risk of losing their jobs. (although)

9. There is still no miracle cure for cancer. Scientists are making real progress. (nevertheless)

10. Most cancer is due to the environment. Heredity is also an important factor. (though)

ADDITIONAL WRITING TOPICS

1. Research the causes of a health problem such as heart disease, high blood pressure, stress, or obesity. What can be done to avoid or control these problems?
2. Research the main causes of *one* kind of pollution, such as air pollution, water pollution, noise pollution, or acid rain. What can realistically be done to reduce this kind of pollution?
3. Choose a topic from economics or business, such as unemployment, inflation, underdevelopment, or the price of goods or services. What are *some* of the factors influencing your topic? These questions are complicated: Do not try to explain everything.
4. Write an essay, imagining you are a high school teacher trying to explain a scientific topic simply. Sample topics might be ocean waves, a rainbow, a dying star, chemical bonding, the structure of an atom.
5. Choose *one* area in which the United States has had an important influence on your country. You might choose an area such as one of these: politics, business, education, popular culture, art. How has this influence affected your country: Do you feel this influence has been positive, negative, or both?
6. The average American child watches enormous amounts of television. How do you think this might influence the child's personality or his or her way of understanding the world? Many articles have been written on this topic if you wish to do research.

Lesson Ten

ARGUING A POSITION

Subject: Population Growth

Contents:

INTRODUCTION

This lesson, like the last one, involves research into a problem—rapid population growth—and a consideration of causes and results. You will consider two general approaches to the problem, one involving voluntary birth control, the other involuntary birth control, and decide which you think is more acceptable and effective. You will then argue the position you have chosen.

In Cycle One, to become familiar with the problem, you will analyze some statistics on world population growth and consider some of the factors known to reduce population growth.

In Cycle Two a specific, and controversial, way to reduce population growth is proposed. You must decide whether you agree or disagree with the proposal, whether you support it or not. Once you have chosen a position, you will organize into teams to plan your arguments and your library research. This section concludes with a debate and an essay on the topic of involuntary birth control.

Adding On provides practice in advanced grammar and complex paragraph development.

CYCLE ONE

Practice 1. The Nature of the Problem: Some Statistics

Exercise A   *For thousands of years world population grew slowly. Social and economic conditions were such that nearly as many people died each year as were born. Then, about four hundred years ago, conditions began to improve and more people were born each year than died. This simple fact has had a tremendous effect on population. To get an idea of the rate of growth and the numbers involved, plot the following data concerning world population at different dates on Figure 10-1 and answer the questions which follow.*

Year	Population
1	.3 billion
1650	.5 billion
1850	1.1 billion
1950	2.5 billion
1985	4.8 billion
2000	6.1 billion
2025	8.2 billion

1. How much did world population increase between the years 1 and 1650? Between 1650 and 1950? How much will it have increased between 1950 and 2025?

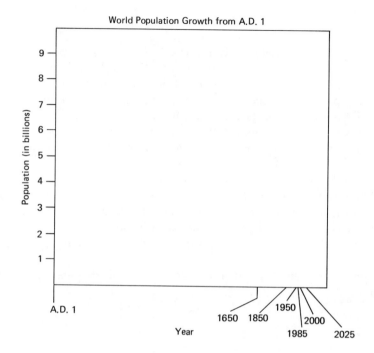

Sources: 1 A.D.–1850, *The World Almanac and Book of Facts*, 1984.
1950–2025, United Nations, *World Population Prospects as Assessed in 1980*, 1981.

Figure 10-1

2. Do you understand why the increase is greater each time even though the period is shorter?

Exercise B   *It is important to understand not only that population grows but also why it grows at the rate you saw in Figure 10-1. It is important to understand, in other words, why the line rises so sharply in Figure 10-1. This can be clearly understood by considering a simplified situation: Imagine a society in which each couple has exactly six children, who eventually marry and have six children, and so on. Calculate the number of children in each of the first five generations and plot this data on Figure 10-2. The number of couples in a generation will be half the number of children in the preceding generation. These data do not reflect real population growth because they do not consider the number of deaths in relation to the number of births. Nevertheless, they will make clear the dynamics of accelerating growth.*

	Generation	**Couples**	**× 6 =**	**Total Children**
	1	1,000	× 6	6,000
Ex:	2	3,000	× 6	18,000
	3		× 6	
	4		× 6	
	5		× 6	

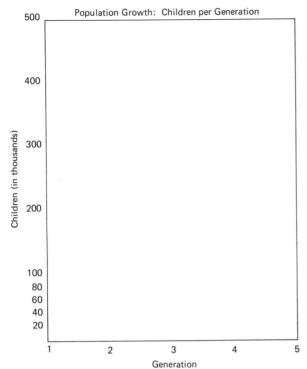

Children (in thousands)

Population Growth: Children per Generation

Generation

Figure 10-2

Source: U.S. Bureau of the Census, *Current Population Reports*, Series P-20,
no. 373 and P-23, no. 130.

Exercise C   *To understand the true nature of the problem, it is important to consider not only the numbers but also the social conditions that cause the rate of population growth to differ dramatically in different parts of the world. The statistics in Table 10-1 make these regional differences clear. Answer the questions following Table 10-1.*

Table 10-1   Population Growth by Year 2000

REGION	POPULATION (IN MILLIONS)		INCREASE
	1980	2000	
Europe	488	511	5%
North America	256	286	12%
China	1,000	1,200	20%
Asia	1,671	2,328	39%
Latin America	378	549	45%
Africa	498	847	70%

1. Why do you think Europe, North America, and Japan (which is not shown separately) have low birthrates?

2. What is the poorest region in the world? Which region has the highest birthrate?

3. What is the relation between poverty and population growth?

4. What might be some of the reasons the poor have large families?

5. Do you have any idea why the birthrate in China—a poor country—is so much lower than in the rest of Asia?

Practice 2. Reading: Social Conditions and Population Growth

The last exercise made it clear that there is a relation between economic develop-ment and population growth. The following essay goes into the connection in more detail and will introduce you to some of the ideas important to a discussion of population control. Notice also that the essay is documented in the way pre-sented in Lesson 9, Practice 4. Questions follow the essay.

SOCIAL CONDITIONS AND POPULATION GROWTH

1

5

10

Modernized countries once had fertility rates as high as those of present-day developing countries, but as these countries industrialized, birthrates fell. This change from high fertility (birthrates of 40 or more per 1,000) to low fertility (birthrates of 20 or under per 1,000) is known as "demographic transition" (Easterlin 1983, 564). The purpose of this paper is to consider the factors involved in demographic transition and to ask whether such a transition is possible in premodern, or developing, countries.

One of the points most often made is that there is a relation between urbanization and low fertility. All developed countries, coun-tries which have low birthrates, are highly urbanized. In almost all coun-tries, furthermore, fertility is lower in the cities than in the countryside (Weinstein 1976, 68–69). This difference in fertility is probably related to the differences between a modern urban economy and a traditional agricultural economy. In an agricultural economy children are valuable as a source of labor and as old-age insurance for their parents (Potter 1983, 639). They can begin to work on the land and around the house at an early age and they will take care of their parents when they get old. For these reasons peasants probably value large families.

In a modern urban economy, on the other hand, children do not usually work and they are more expensive to raise. Food must be bought rather than raised; clothes may be bought rather than made. People working in the modern economic sector may also be less dependent on their children for support in old age than agricultural workers. They may have savings, or receive government assistance, when they no longer work (Potter 1983, 639). Finally, urban life offers a greater choice of goods and activities than rural life. A couple living in a city may choose to limit family size in order to be able to afford or to do other things (Easterlin 1983, 572). Peasants may not have this choice.

Although it is true that birthrates are generally lower in cities than in rural areas, it is important to understand that urbanization by itself is not an answer to the problem of overpopulation. It is the combination of urbanization and modern economic activity that dramatically lowers the birthrate. This can be seen from the fact that some highly urbanized countries, for example, Mexico, Colombia, and Iraq, have high birthrates because in these countries many of the people living in cities are not integrated into the modern economy. As Weinstein (1976, 92) puts it, "Throughout the third world, a high proportion of urban dwellers maintain peasant life styles and, even, agricultural occupations."

Improved health and education, likewise products of modernization, are also clearly related to reduced fertility. When child mortality rates decline, the birthrate declines also (Watson et al. 1979, 161). It may be somewhat surprising that family size eventually becomes smaller as fewer children die. However, if parents are confident that most of their children will survive, they plan to have fewer. In other words, they will not try to have as many as possible to ensure that some will survive.

Education is even more directly linked to fertility: The higher the level of education, the lower the birthrate. Indeed, literacy seems to be more clearly related to reduced fertility than any other single factor (Freedman 1973, 185). Education may reduce fertility by introducing people to nontraditional ideas and ways of thinking: "With increased education and literacy the population becomes involved with ideas and institutions of larger modern culture" (Freedman 1973, 185). This "larger modern culture" may be primarily the culture of the Western middle class, which values low fertility (Caldwell 1980, 228). Schools may also influence fertility by teaching students that they have a duty not only to the family but also to the larger society, the country, which would benefit from reduced population growth (Caldwell 1980, 228).

Another factor which is crucial to understanding fertility is the status of women, both in the family and in the society. In many traditional societies a woman's role is defined exclusively in terms of moth-

65 erhood, and her status depends on how well she fulfills this role. In such societies women tend to have many children (Oppong and Haavio-Mannila 1979, 462). However, when women begin to work outside the home, at least in modern-sector urban jobs, fertility begins to decline (Oppong and Haavio-Mannila 1979, 466). First, modern-sector jobs require a woman to work away from her family, making it more difficult to care

70 for a large family, especially where the family structure is nuclear rather than extended. Such work also broadens the conception of what a woman's role is, offering alternative sources of recognition and status (Beckman 1983, 431). For this reason, women working in modern-sector urban jobs usually come to have more power in the family and more say in

75 decision making. This power, in turn, has an important effect on fertility because women tend to want fewer children than men (Beckman 1983, 434).

The factors discussed so far—urbanization, the modern economy, health, education, the status of women—seem to be clearly related

80 to the process of demographic transition in those countries where it has occurred naturally, the more developed countries. The question is whether this type of transition can be expected to occur in less-developed countries, that is, whether modernization is an answer to the population problems of the poorer countries of the world. Or to put the

85 question differently: Can less-developed countries seriously reduce population growth without first becoming modern industrial societies?

In at least two important ways countries in early stages of economic development cannot be compared to the now-developed countries when they began the process of modernization and demographic

90 transition. First, the less-developed countries are already crowded and growing at extremely rapid rates, whereas most of the more-developed countries, the United States and the countries of Western Europe, at any rate, did not face such pressure from population growth when they began to modernize. Rapid population growth by itself may make it

95 difficult for countries to modernize. In other words, population growth may be so great that it will make it difficult to achieve the kind of modernization which almost automatically lowers the birthrate (McNamara 1984, 1109).

The second difference is a more positive or hopeful one. Less-

100 developed countries possess modern communication systems such as did not exist in the preindustrial West, and these communication networks allow the rapid spread of ideas and models for living (Freedman 1979, 67). Specifically, the poor are aware of the way of life in the more-developed countries and aspire to that way of life themselves. They may

105 well understand that it is necessary to reduce population growth in order for them, or their children, to improve their standard of living. Even in preindustrial societies, in other words, the idea that fewer can live better may be enough to change reproductive behavior.

While stressing the important role of ideas or alternate models

110 for living in reducing population growth, Freedman also recognizes the importance of modernization. He points out, however, that it is not

necessary for a country to be fully modernized for the birthrate to fall considerably (1979, 66). He feels the following conditions may be suffi-cient: better health, higher education for both boys and girls, welfare institutions which decrease the dependence of parents on children, com-munication and transportation networks. A number of partially mod-ernized countries with strong family planning programs, such as China, Thailand, and Indonesia, have been able to reduce fertility significantly (Freedman 1979, 66).

It is not clear, however, that the conditions outlined by Freed-man are always adequate. Although population growth has slowed down in China and Indonesia, it remains largely unchanged in much of Africa, South Asia, and Latin America. In countries such as Pakistan and Bangladesh, serious government programs have had little effect. Ac-cording to McNamara (1984, 1,136) 1.1 billion people live in countries where fertility decline has not even begun. The failure of population control programs in such countries leads McNamara (1984, 1,120) to fear that:

> Restraints on reproductive freedom may become . . . more common in cases where governments through incapacity or unawareness have al-lowed demographic pressures to build to extremes. I am not speaking here of government measures aimed at creating greater social responsi-bility in the reproductive decisions made by families, but of coercive government intrusions into the decision themselves—forced steriliza-tion for example.

In summary, although the conditions leading to reduced fertility have been a subject of intense study, and some understanding of these conditions has been gained, there is still no certain or guaranteed way to reduce fertility in developing countries. Programs that have been suc-cessful in some countries have not worked in others. In some countries fertility is falling with little government interference, whereas in others governments spend millions of dollars with little effect. It can only be hoped that further efforts will meet with more consistent success.

References

Beckman, Linda J. 1983. "Communication, Power, and the Influence of Social Networks in Couple Decisions on Fertility." In Bulatao and Lee 415–43.

Bulatao, A., and Ronald D. Lee, Ed. 1983. *Determinants of Fertility in Developing Countries: Fertility Regulation and Institutional Influences.* New York: Academic Press.

Caldwell, J. C. 1980. "Mass Education as a Determinant of the Timing of Fertil-ity Decline." *Population and Development Review* 6: 225–55.

Easterlin, Richard A. 1983. "Modernization and Fertility: A Critical Essay." In Bulatao and Lee 562–86.

Freedman, Ronald. 1973. "Norms for Family Size in Underdeveloped Areas." *Population, Environment and Social Organization: Current Issues in Human Ecology.* Ed. M. Micklin. Hinsdale, Ill: The Dryden Press. 171–94.

Freedman, Ronald. 1979. "Theories of Fertility Decline: A Reappraisal." In Hauser 63–79.

Hauser, Philip M., Ed. 1979. *World Population and Development: Challenges and Prospects.* Syracuse, N.Y.: Syracuse UP.

McNamara, Robert S. 1984. "Time Bomb or Myth: The Population Problem." *Foreign Affairs* 62: 1,107–31.

Oppong, Christine, and Elina Haavio-Mannila. 1979. "Women, Population, and Development." In Hauser 440–85.

Potter, Joseph E. 1983. "Effects of Societal and Community Institutions on Fertility." In Bulatao and Lee 627–65.

Watson, Walter, Allan Rosenfield, Mechai Viravaidya, and Krasae Chana-wongse. 1979. "Health, Population, and Nutrition: Interrelations, Problems, and Possible Solutions." In Hauser 145–73.

Weinstein, Jay A. 1976. *Demographic Transition and Social Change.* Morristown, N.J.: General Learning Press.

Questions

1. What does "a birthrate of 40 or more per 1,000" mean?
2. What would be a typical birthrate for a country that has undergone "demographic transition"?
3. What questions is this paper going to deal with (lines 5–8)?
4. What evidence is given to support the idea that birthrates are lower in cities than in the countryside (lines 10–15)?
5. Why is the birthrate high in agricultural communities (lines 15–19)?
6. What are the three reasons given for the lower birthrate in cities (lines 20–29)?
7. Do all urbanized countries have low birthrates (lines 30–41)?
8. What is the relation between child mortality and the birthrate (lines 42–48)?
9. What reasons are given to explain the relation between education and lower birthrates (lines 49–60)?
10. Who would be likely to have fewer children, a woman working in agriculture or a woman working in a department store (lines 61–77)? Why?
11. Does rapid population growth make modernization easier (lines 87–98)?
12. What is the role of modern communication in lowering birthrates (lines 99–108)?
13. Have any developing countries lowered their birthrates (lines 116–119)?
14. Are population control programs always successful (lines 120–124)?

Practice 3. Possible Measures

In the preceding exercise you read about the general relation between social conditions and population growth. The following exercise presents some rather specific measures which might be effective in reducing population growth. Rank them according to how effective you think they would be and then write sentences expressing your opinions. You can indicate how certain you feel by your choice of modal (Lesson 4, Practice 11):

    a.   A publicity campaign <u>could</u> (or <u>might, would</u>) lower the birthrate.

Or you might use the *it* + *be* + adjective pattern (Lesson 8, Practice 10). Notice that a modal is also used in this pattern:

b.   It is possible (or probable, unlikely, and so on) that a publicity campaign would lower the birthrate.

A number of adverbs, most related to the adjectives in pattern b, can also be used to express degree of certainty. Notice that a modal is again necessary and that these adverbs can take more than one position in the sentence:

c.   Possibly, a publicity campaign would lower the birthrate.
(or) A publicity campaign might possibly lower the birthrate.

The adverbs most commonly used in this pattern are *possibly, probably, clearly, surely, undoubtedly, certainly.*

Exercise   *Rank the measures in the following list from 1 to 4 (1 = very effective; 4 = very ineffective). Then write sentences expressing your opinions. You may want to explain your thinking also. Keep in mind that these measures would be applied in developing countries; you are not deciding whether these measures would be effective in already developed countries.*

Ex: 1.   __4__ television publicity campaign
A television publicity campaign would clearly do little good: Poor people in developing countries do not have televisions.

2.   _____ radio programs on family planning

3.   _____ radio publicity suggesting people move to cities

4.   _____ government education teams in the countryside

5.   _____ explaining family planning in elementary school

6.   _____ teaching birth control in high school

7.   _____ publicity suggesting people reduce sexual activity

8.   _____ giving marriage licenses only to women 25 and older

9. ＿＿＿ requiring parents have a "baby permit"

10. ＿＿＿ lowering taxes for small families

11. ＿＿＿ linking family size to better housing and employment

12. ＿＿＿ easily available free abortion

CYCLE TWO

Practice 4. Debate/Composition Topic

It is a matter of debate whether voluntary methods of lowering population growth will work fast enough. Some experts fear that if a huge effort is not made in the next few years, many governments will be forced to begin programs of involuntary birth control.

The proposal that follows is a controversial one, but one that governments may have to face. Decide if you agree or disagree with this proposal:

> The social changes necessary to reduce population growth cannot be made fast enough to prevent disastrous population growth. Voluntary birth control programs will not take effect soon enough. Therefore, governments should begin programs of required or involuntary birth control. Such programs might require abortion or sterilization after the birth of a couple's second child. Group survival is more important than individual freedom.

When you have made up your minds, that is, decided on your positions, divide into groups or opposing teams to plan your arguments and your library research. If each member of a group finds one relevant article and reports back to the group, you will have quite a lot of information about population growth. Look especially for information on actual birth control programs in developing countries. Are they succeeding or failing? How has China reduced the birthrate?

To argue *against* the idea of involuntary birth control, you will have to argue that the problem is not as serious as it seems or that there are alternatives which will work. Look for information on countries with effective birth control programs. You might also argue that involuntary birth control programs would not work, that they would be ineffective.

To argue *for* involuntary birth control, you will have to maintain that it would, in fact, work and that it is the only thing that would work fast enough.

Note: To debate, or to write argumentation, you must anticipate the arguments of those who may disagree with you: the debater on the other team or your reader. Be ready to answer these objections.

Practice 5. Readings: For and Against

The following readings could be used to support opposite positions in the debate. The first argues that the problems which rapid growth will cause in the near future will be unmanageable. The second argues that the rate of world population growth is already slowing down.

GLOBAL POPULATION—A GLIMPSE INTO THE FUTURE*

1   146 a minute, 8,700 an hour, 210,950 a day, and 77 million a year.

Those are the numbers by which the human race—now at 4.6 billion people—is expanding despite wars, starvation, birth control ad-
5   vances and overcrowding. Furthermore, recent studies suggest that little change in the pattern can be expected until next century. The implications of new population projections by the United Nations and the Population Reference Bureau are frightening:

By far the fastest expansion is occurring in the poor, less devel-
10   oped nations—the very places where food, housing, sanitation and economic opportunity are already in shortest supply. Africa's population, for instance, could double in less than 25 years.

Based on present trends, the earliest that the world could expect zero growth (when deaths equal births) is the year 2040 at 8 billion
15   people, say U.N. experts. The more likely year is 2110 at 10.5 billion. It is even possible the balance might not arrive until 2130 at more than 14 billion.

Social and political pressures are likely to increase as migrations to urban areas continue. Mexico City, already huge at 15 million, will
20   have twice as many people by the year 2000, predicts the U.N. By the close of this century, more than half of the world's population will live in large cities.

Questions
1. Are the statistics in this article from reliable sources? What are they?
2. Do the projections in this article take into account birth control programs?
3. According to this article, when will world population growth stop? What will the total population be at that time?
4. If the population doubles, what will life be like in areas which are already short of food, jobs, housing, and sanitation?

*Reprinted from *U.S. News and World Report;* Copyright, 1982, U.S. News and World Report, Inc. Aug. 2, 1982.

5. What social, political, and environmental problems will result from such rapid growth?

6. How might population growth increase conflict between groups and nations?

WORLD POPULATION DECLINE DOCUMENTED*

1   Last year Harvard University's Center for Population Studies reported that the world's population growth rate has begun to decline and this year similar findings are reported by the World Fertility Survey.
5   Population growth is declining in 14 of the 15 developing countries studied in the survey.

This conclusion was reached by comparing the number of children women 45 to 49 have had with the number of children all women in their reproductive years expect to have. In Costa Rica, for example, women aged 45–49 have had an average of 7.2 live births during their
10   lives, but younger women are now expected to average only 3.8 births by the time they reach the same age. In Sri Lanka, women aged 45 to 49 had an average of 6.0 live births, but women of reproductive age are now expected to have only 3.4 births by the time they reach their late 40s, an equally sharp decline. Somewhat less dramatic drops can also be
15   seen in South Korea, Fiji, Indonesia, Panama, Colombia, Malaysia and Thailand.

According to the survey, there are several reasons why the birthrate is falling in these 14 countries. For one, women in the 14 countries are marrying later than they used to. For another, they are more in-
20   terested than women of previous generations were in limiting the size of their families. In fact, a two-child family is even becoming the ideal for many of these women. A third reason that birthrates are falling in these 14 countries is that more and more women of reproductive age are using modern methods of birth control. In fact, the degree of decline in the
25   birthrate seems to be closely related to the number of women using contraceptives. For instance, in Costa Rica, where the birthrate has been reduced dramatically, 78 percent of the women are using contraception.

Questions
1. Are the sources of the information in this article reliable?
2. Explain the method used in determining the decline in birthrate.
3. Why is the birthrate declining?
4. Does this article disprove the statistics in the preceding reading?

Practice 6. Directed Writing: Controlling Population Growth

After researching and debating the topic, write an essay agreeing or disagreeing with the idea that involuntary birth control is the only way to reduce population growth fast enough. Be sure to take into consideration the objections of those

*Reprinted with permission from *Science News*, the weekly newsmagazine of science, copyright 1979 by Science Service, Inc. Aug. 4, 1979.

who would disagree with you; in other words, do not assume the reader agrees with you. The following are possible ways to organize this essay:

If You Agree	If You Disagree
Background: the seriousness of the problem; the need for real progress, soon.	You will probably agree the problem is serious but you may question how soon it will become a crisis.
Why you think other possible solutions would not work fast enough. Consider alternative solutions seriously.	Why involuntary birth control would not work: religious, cultural, moral, or political objections.
Answer religious, cultural, moral, or political objections. Argue that involuntary birth control would work.	Why other programs could be successful; describe an "ideal" population control for a developing country.

ADDING ON

Practice 7. Using Concession and Contrast to Express Disagreement

Certain concession and contrast signals can be used to express not only unexpectedness (Lesson 9, Practice 9) but also disagreement. One person might argue that it is necessary to improve a country's standard of living in order to reduce the birthrate but another person might not agree that this is a practical solution to the problem. This disagreement might be expressed as follows:

a. <u>Although</u> it is true a higher standard of living would lower the birth rate, economic development is a long, slow process.

b. It is true a higher standard of living would lower the birth rate; economic development, <u>however</u>, is a long, slow process.

To write argumentation you must consider opposing viewpoints even if you reject them: These sentence patterns can be used to do just that. The signals most often used in this way are: *though, although, while, however, but.*

Exercise *Using the information cues below, write sentences of concession/disagreement. The cues are meant to suggest an idea for a sentence; you do not have to use the exact words given.*

	Concession	**Disagreement**
1.	later marriage . . . effective . . . China	requires government control of citizens
Ex:	<u>Although encouraging later marriage has been effective in China, it requires too much government control over people's lives</u>.	
2.	"child tax" . . . interesting idea	not realistic to tax the very poor
3.	true: abortion effective	medical services inadequate in developing countries

4. equality for women reduces births   difficult to change cultural attitudes
5. certain: education effective   take many years
6. sterilization . . . end large families   morally, culturally unacceptable
7. world birthrate high   falling significantly
8. sterilization may seem easy   result: political violence

Practice 8. Expressing Condition

Conditional sentences such as those below would be very natural in an essay considering approaches to the population problem:

   a. If contraceptives <u>are</u> available, people <u>will use</u> them.

   b. If a government <u>began</u> a program of involuntary sterilization, there <u>would be</u> political violence.

You can see from these examples that the choice of verb tense in conditional sentences is complicated. It depends not only on time (both of these sentences refer to the future) but on the person's attitude toward the situation described. As you saw in Lesson Four, Practice 11, a future situation can be viewed as either realistic—one that may actually exist—or hypothetical—one that is unrealistic and will probably never exist. The grammar in sentence *a* indicates that the situation is viewed as a realistic one, whereas the grammar in *b* indicates that the situation is a hypothetical one: The writer does not think programs of involuntary sterilization will be tried.

    Conditional sentences consist of two clauses, a clause of condition (the *if* clauses in the examples above) and a clause of result. If the future situation is viewed as a realistic one, the verb in the clause of condition is in a present tense and one of the following modals (indicating degree of certainty) is used in the clause of result: *could, might, may, should, will.* If the future situation is a hypothetical one, the verb in the clause of condition is in a past tense and one of the following modals is used in the clause of result: *could, might, would.*

    Finally, *if* is not the only *condition signal.* Others are: *only if, even if, whether or not, provided that, unless.* They are all combining signals:

   c. People will have fewer children <u>only if</u> they are better educated.

   d. <u>Even if</u> governments raised the legal age for marrying, it might not make much difference.

   e. Peasants might prefer large families <u>whether or not</u> they are educated in the use of birth control.

   f. The poor will use contraception <u>provided that</u> it is free and available.

   g. <u>Unless</u> governments were willing to use force, involuntary sterilization would not work.

Exercise *Fill in the blanks in the following sentences with a modal or the correct form of the verb given in parentheses. The grammar should be realistic or hypothetical as indicated.*

Ex: 1. People ____would____ learn how to use contraceptives if special education teams ____were____ (be) sent into the countryside. (hypothetical)

2. If women _____ (have) greater equality, they _____ have fewer children. (hypothetical)

3. If the high rate of infant mortality _____ (be) reduced, the poor _____ have smaller families because they _____ be confident that most of their children _____ survive. (realistic)

4. If the population _____ (continue) to grow at the present rate, there _____ be even greater suffering in poor countries. (realistic)

5. There are so many young people in the world now that the population _____ not stabilize for years even if everyone _____ (start) having only two children immediately. (hypothetical)

6. Educational radio programs _____ work provided that enough people _____ (have) radios. (realistic)

7. If developed countries _____ (increase) aid to developing countries, birth control programs _____ start to make real progress. (hypothetical)

8. If family size _____ (be) reduced, children _____ (receive) better care. (hypothetical)

Practice 9. Noun Clauses

A full clause preceded by the words *the fact that* can function as a noun: as a subject or as an object of either a verb or a preposition:

a. The fact that they provide free labor makes children an important resource in a poor agricultural society. (subject)

b. Most people are not aware of the fact that world population could double in thirty or forty years. (object of preposition)

The word *fact* is not the only one that can be used in this construction, though it is the most common one. A couple of other examples are:

c. The suggestion that the poor are too ignorant to understand birth control is false. (subject)

d. Many people reject the idea that the government can decide family size. (object of verb)

Exercise *Complete the following sentences, using noun clauses of the type just presented. In Part **A,** cue words suggest how you might complete the sentences; the key word (for example, **fact**) is italicized. In Part **B,** finish the sentences any way that makes sense.*

A 1. (*fact:* China . . . two-child family) shows that dramatic reductions in family size are possible.

  Ex: <u>The fact that China has achieved the goal of the two-child family</u> shows that dramatic reductions in family size are possible.

  (Or) <u>The fact that the average family in China now has fewer than two children</u> shows that dramatic reductions in family size are possible.

  2. Many, nevertheless, are very disturbed by (*fact:* China's program . . . individual has little choice)

  3. (*possibility:* . . . involuntary measures . . . necessary in the future) is one that worries many people.

  4. (*fact:* some religions oppose abortion) is an extremely important consideration in planning a population control program.

  5. A number of cultural attitudes, such as (*idea:* necessary . . . at least one son), make it difficult to reduce the birthrate in traditional societies.

B 6. _____ makes literacy programs an important part of population control.

  7. Some governments in developing countries consider population control a low priority despite _____.

  8. People who seriously propose involuntary sterilization ignore _____.

  9. _____ makes the radio more effective than the newspaper as a means of educating people.

Practice 10. Complex Paragraph Development

As you saw in Lesson 9, Practice 7, advanced writers use a variety of methods to develop their ideas, to make their meaning clear and convincing. In the following short essays the ideas are not adequately developed. Following the essays are questions which should help you add development where indicated by the blanks. You may choose to develop the first essay, which argues *for* involuntary birth control, or the second, which argues *against* it.

THE CASE FOR INVOLUNTARY BIRTH CONTROL

Although involuntary birth control would be drastic and perhaps dangerous, it is the only solution with any real chance of succeeding. Voluntary programs do not work fast enough. To begin with, most poor people want to have large families. __(1)__

People who are opposed to involuntary birth control will say that such ways of thinking can be changed by education, but education is slow and expensive. Even if the money were available now to begin serious education in birth control, it would be years before the birthrate could be significantly reduced. __(2)__

It is also unrealistic to think that third world governments can control population growth by such means as taxing large families, raising the marriage age, or issuing "baby permits." __(3)__

Questions
1. Why do poor people want large families? Because of ignorance? Religious reasons? The usefulness of children? The fear that many may die? The desire to have male children?
2. What would the results of waiting be? Can you give a statistic? How would this affect the standard of living? The food supply? Employment possibilities? The environment? Political stability?
3. Why wouldn't these ideas work? Variations on these ideas have been used in China with considerable success. How is China different from other third world countries?

THE CASE AGAINST INVOLUNTARY BIRTH CONTROL

It may be true that voluntary birth control programs are expensive and require some time to take effect. There is, however, no choice. Forced birth control would never work because it would never be accepted. __(1)__

Moreover, it is not true that voluntary birth control programs do not work. __(2)__ This success is possible because the poor readily accept birth control if it is made available to them. They clearly understand that the quality of life will be improved if family size is reduced. __(3)__

Population control programs will work if people are educated in the use of birth control and given clear incentives to reduce family size. The cost of educating people in the use of birth control should not be exaggerated. What is required in the short term is not general education for everyone but well-focused, specific programs. __(4)__

With regard to incentives to reduce family size, it is important to understand that people can be rewarded for having small families more easily and more effectively than they can be punished for having large ones. In other words, there are very effective alternatives to such things as "child taxes" and "baby permits." __(5)__

Questions
1. Why would people reject it? Religious, cultural, political reasons? What might be possible political consequences of forced birth control?
2. Can you give one or two examples of countries with successful population control programs? Any statistics?
3. Can you restate this idea or perhaps give examples of how the "quality of life" might be improved?
4. Can you describe a short-term program in birth control? What would have to be taught? What means could be used? Radio? Traveling education teams?
5. Can you give an example of an economic "reward" for limiting family size?

Practice 11. Review of Signal Expressions

In an essay developed by a variety of means, a variety of signal expressions may be used. In each part of the following essay, fill in the blanks with the signal expressions given in the margin. Each one will be used once. In some cases there may be some freedom in the order in which they are used.

POPULATION CONTROL: SOCIAL, CULTURAL, AND RELIGIOUS ATTITUDES

Part I
indeed
√ first
if
in other words
moreover
for this reason

Ex: 1. For a population control program to work, it must take into consideration the social, cultural, and religious attitudes of the people involved. _____First_____, it should be remembered that children have a social role. People do not have children only for the pleasure of raising them. In an agricultural society, they may be

2. important, _____ necessary, to the family economy, which relies on hands, not machines. Chil-

3. dren are, _____, the only type of "social security" in most agricultural societies. In such societies, people expect to be cared for by their children when

4. they grow old. _____, the typical peasant may

5. hesitate to have a small family. _____ a peasant couple has only one or two children, and those children do not survive, the parents may not be pro-

6. vided for in their old age. _____, there is security in numbers.

Part II
because
in fact
until
nevertheless
for example

Another cultural factor to consider is the relative status of men and women, or male children and female

7. children. _____ male children are more highly esteemed in many societies, a couple may not wish to

8. stop having children _____ they have at least one son. This cultural attitude is very deep-rooted.

Part III
for instance
however
even if
another
that is
to give one example

9. _____, in countries with strict population pro-
10. grams, _____ China, there is some evidence that female babies are not as well cared for as male babies. Some observers think the mortality rate is higher for female infants than for male infants. It is not
11. certain this is true. _____, the problem is a real one, one which must be considered.
12. _____ crucial factor, of course, is religious belief. Many religions place great value on large fami-
13. lies. The Bible, _____, says, "Go forth and
14,15. multiply," _____, have children. _____ people become convinced that they should have smaller families, religious beliefs influence the type of population control programs that are possible. In Catho-
16. lic countries, _____, required abortion is religiously and culturally unthinkable: The Catholic church is strongly opposed to abortion.

Problems such as these make it clear that the solution
17. to population growth will not be easy. _____, the fact that successful birth control programs do exist shows that the situation is not hopeless.

ADDITIONAL WRITING TOPICS

Write an essay either agreeing or disagreeing with one of the following proposals.

1. A controversial theory maintains that the richer nations should not help poorer nations fight hunger and starvation by sending food or money. According to this theory, such aid only postpones the problem and makes it worse because it allows the hungry to survive, and reproduce, thus increasing the number of people who will be hungry in the future. Do you agree that the rich should allow starvation? Note: To understand the thinking behind this theory, you should probably do some research: It is known as the "lifeboat theory."
2. Women should have the same military duties as men if they want the same rights in other areas of life.
3. Countries which possess nuclear technology should not export it to developing nations because this increases the threat to world peace.
4. All nations should agree to an immediate freeze on the development of nuclear weapons.
5. The United States provides relatively inexpensive higher education to a very high proportion of its population. This is a waste of the public's money because many students do not really profit from a college education and their contribution to society does not justify the expense of their education.
6. Many foreign students remain in the United States after they receive their degrees. In this way, many developing nations lose some of their most highly trained citizens. Foreign students should be required to return to their native

countries to work for a period when they finish their studies in the United States.

7. Modern medical technology makes it possible to predict several kinds of birth defects. Should the government require all people to have such tests? Should people who are in danger of having children with birth defects be allowed to have children?

8. Abortion should be made illegal except when the mother's life is in danger.

INDEX